Change is the Third Path

A Workbook for Ending Abusive and Violent Behavior

Michael Lindsey

Robert W. McBride

Constance M. Platt

GYLANTIC PUBLISHING COMPANY
Littleton, Colorado

To order additional copies:

GYLANTIC PUBLISHING COMPANY
P.O. Box 2792
Littleton, Colorado 80161-2792
1-800-828-0113 Fax: 727-4279 E-mail: GylanP@aol.com
For orders of less than four books, please add $2.00 for shipping and handling.

Printed in the United States of America by Gilliland Printing, Inc.
The text is printed with soy ink.

International Standard Book Number: 1-880197-14-6

Acknowledgment

Many people have worked long and hard in the domestic violence movement to stop the abuse, save lives, and inform the public. These people often receive little or no appreciation for their difficult and stressful work. This is dedicated to them. Thank you.

In a few instances, we have adapted pieces of material from handouts that have traveled through the mental health community with no creator identification.

Table of Contents

Using This Book

This book is a tool for you to use with a therapist. Working on your own and using this book by itself will provide you with only limited help. The information and exercises are meant to:

> challenge your ideas, allow you to think about how you live your life, provide you with thoughts for discussion in group therapy, and help you develop skills to improve your life.

Hopefully you will choose to be honest with yourself and with others with whom you share what you have learned.

Each exercise has a set of directions. As you work the exercise, ask yourself what each part means to you and how it applies to you. Ask yourself if you are really being truthful or are kidding yourself. These are not pass or fail quizzes. The only person you would be fooling is yourself.

Most of us want the same things in our lives. You want to have positive relationships with the people you know and to feel successful and satisfied with what you do to make a living. You want to provide yourself and your family with material things and to be loved and be able to give love. You have tried to accomplish these things and may have had some success. For all the times that you have tried, ask yourself how often you come away from your effort feeling frustrated, misunderstood, used, beaten, hurt, or angry.

You may expect the "world" to work according to your agenda and are disappointed when it doesn't. You may also expect the world to be fair and reasonable. The world has not, is not, and will not be fair and reasonable and to think it will change for your agenda is a mistake. If you feel as though the "system"—relationships, jobs, courts, etc.—keep running over you like a steam roller, it is time to look at the choices you make and the way in which you deal with the world. Why keep fighting the world and getting run-over? You will eventually destroy yourself in the process. It takes work but you can find how to make your life satisfying.

Ask yourself a couple of questions:

Is my life working for me or is it a struggle?
Is my life satisfying and rewarding or do I feel confused and cheated?

The diagram below is a basic description of your situation. The system is going to contain your behavior which it sees as unacceptable. Your goal or agenda has been to resist containment and maintain the beliefs and behaviors you know, whether or not they work for you. Starting now with this book you will begin to examine your agenda on a regular basis. Men entering treatment for battering behavior usually have the agenda described in the following diagram.

Containment

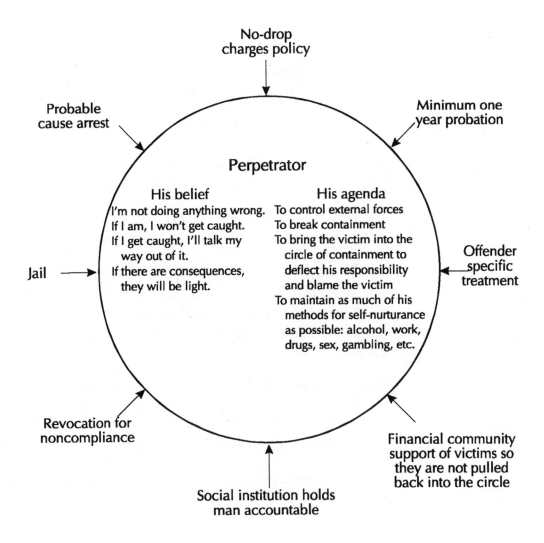

Perpetrator

His belief
I'm not doing anything wrong.
If I am, I won't get caught.
If I get caught, I'll talk my way out of it.
If there are consequences, they will be light.

His agenda
To control external forces
To break containment
To bring the victim into the circle of containment to deflect his responsibility and blame the victim
To maintain as much of his methods for self-nurturance as possible: alcohol, work, drugs, sex, gambling, etc.

No-drop charges policy

Probable cause arrest

Minimum one year probation

Jail

Offender specific treatment

Revocation for noncompliance

Social institution holds man accountable

Financial community support of victims so they are not pulled back into the circle

Change is the Third Path
M. Lindsey, R. McBride and C. Platt

2

If there is to be any chance for you to make positive changes in your life and to develop a new and constructive set of values and skills, you will need to surrender to and accept the idea that your life is unmanageable and that you are powerless to make changes without help. This concept taken from Alcoholics Anonymous (AA) clearly defines a necessary first step for you. You must give up your current agenda and begin to accept outside feedback and control.

The process of change requires taking risks, including the risk of feeling enormous emotional pain. No one can make you take the risks or make the changes except yourself.

Do you want to make changes in your life? To start the process of recovery, you will need to:

Understand what domestic violence is.

Take responsibility for your abuse and violence.

Recognize the chaos in your life.

Acknowledge the consequences of your violence to yourself and others.

Work through your denial and minimization.

Next you will need to begin learning some of the tools you can use and things you can do to understand and control your anger and rage. You will begin to:

Learn to be sensitive to your feelings of anger and how they work in a cycle of destructive interaction.

Learn how to take a Time Out.

Explore the history of your anger and rage.

Get in touch with and examine other feelings.

Among the other things you will begin to learn are:

How you really feel about the events of your life.

How to communicate with people.

How to be assertive rather than passive or aggressive.

How to determine what gives your life value and purpose.

How to build relationships with men and women.

We recommend group therapy combined with individual therapy and couples intervention (not couples counseling). If a group is not available then we recommend individual therapy with couples meetings.

We believe that marital therapy (family or couples counseling) as an exclusive method of intervention with family violence is dangerous for the victim until the perpetrator has been violence- and abuse-free for at least six months and does not blame the victim.

What is Domestic Violence?

Legally domestic violence is the infliction or threat of infliction of any bodily injury or harmful physical contact or the destruction of property or threat thereof as a method of coercion, control, revenge, or punishment upon a person with whom the actor is involved in an intimate relationship.

However, the amount of visible injury is not what defines abusive and violent behavior. In the community-at-large a common definition of domestic violence is:

All behaviors between intimate partners in which one harms, gains, or maintains control over the other person. These include emotional or psychological abuse, destruction of property, and sexual or physical abuse that curtails an individual's personal power or creates an atmosphere of fear and intimidation.

Emotional or psychological abuse

Violence is any behavior that exploits another's vulnerability, insecurity, or character. Such behaviors include continuous degradation, intimidation, manipulation, brainwashing, or control of another's actions to the detriment of the individual.

Insults: constant or extreme criticisms that injure. Insults or constant criticism can debilitate a person's self-confidence.

Rejection: direct or indirect actions or statements that create feelings of unworthiness.

Threats and accusations: direct or indirect statements intended to cause emotional or physical harm or loss. This includes lying about the victim's behavior, attitudes, and emotional state or using emotional blackmail.

Making statements and behaviors that distort reality: saying one thing and meaning or doing something else; acting as if you are ignorant about something you do know; expressing a lie as if it were a known truth; stating good intentions or regrets then not following through. This behavior creates increasing confusion and insecurity in the victim.

Disregarding, ignoring, and neglecting: continually denying requests and needs. The message is that the victim is unimportant and undeserving of fair treatment.

Destruction of property

Destruction of property or pets (often accompanying physical violence) or the threat thereof is a method of coercion, control, revenge, or punishment.

Sexual abuse

Sexual abuse is any non-consenting or sexually exploitative verbal or physical behavior. Previous consent does not imply current consent.

Not asking one's partner about her desire for intercourse or using force, coercion, guilt or manipulation is sexual abuse. The sexual act is considered non-consensual if a person is unable to understand or make an informed decision, for instance, the victim is asleep, drugged, drunk, disabled, incapacitated, too young, too old, dependent upon or afraid of the perpetrator.

Verbal sexual abuse is laughing at another's sexuality or body, making jokes, comments of an offensive or assaultive nature, insults or name-calling about the victim's sexual behavior or preferences.

Physical sexual abuse includes non-consensual penetration (oral, anal, vaginal) of the victim's body, or touching (stroking, kissing, licking, sucking, or using objects) the mouth, anus, genitals, breasts or any other part of the victim's body.

Sexual exploitation is the abuse of trust or power in a relationship in order to engage in a sexual interaction or relationship when one individual is in the care or under the authority of another.

Physical abuse

Physical violence is any physically aggressive behavior, withholding of physical needs, indirect physically harmful behavior, or threat of physical abuse.

These behaviors include but are not limited to hitting, slapping, kicking, choking, scratching, pinching, pulling hair, punching, restraining, pushing, pulling, hitting with objects, stabbing, shooting, drowning, burning.

Withholding of physical needs includes interruption of sleep or meals, denying money, food, transportation or help if a person is hurt or sick, locking another out of the home, refusing to give or rationing of necessities.

Indirect physically harmful behavior includes abusing or injuring children, pets or special property.

Change is the Third Path
M. Lindsey, R. McBride and C. Platt

Facts About Domestic Violence

✔ An estimated 6 million American women are battered each year by their partners (Lee Grant. *Battered*, HBO 1990).

✔ Wife-beating results in more injuries that require medical treatment than rape, auto accidents, and muggings combined (E. Stark and A. Flitcraft, 1987).

✔ A woman is more likely to be assaulted, injured, raped, or killed by a male partner than by any other type of assailant (A. Browne and K. Williams, 1987).

✔ 21% of pregnant women have been battered (E. Stark et al, 1981).

✔ Violence will occur at least once in two-thirds of all marriages (M. Roy, 1982).

✔ Domestic violence occurs among all races and socioeconomic groups (M. A. Schulman, 1979).

✔ Once a woman is victimized by domestic violence, her risk of being victimized again is high. During a six-month time period following an incident of domestic violence, approximately 32% of women are victimized again (P.A. Langan and C.A. Innes, 1986).

✔ Men pay a price for their violence. The cost to men is the opposite of what they believe their violence will bring them. They lose their female partners and children, thousands of dollars (legal fees), their jobs, their freedom, and sometimes their lives (M. Lindsey, KCNC-TV, March 1992).

The following statistics were compiled by the Colorado Domestic Violence Coalition

✔ Of all adult domestic violence cases reported 91% were victimizations of women by their male partners (Bureau of Justice Statistics, 1991).

✔ In 1991, 28% of all female murder victims were slain by their husbands or boyfriends (FBI, *Crime in the United States, 1991*. 1992).

✔ More than 90 women were murdered every week in 1991—9 out of 10 were murdered by men (Majority Staff of the U.S. Senate Judiciary Committee, 1992).

✔ Each year, two million women are *severely* assaulted by their male partners—5,479/day; 228/hour; 3.8/minute; 1 every 15 seconds (M.A. Straus & R.J. Gelles, 1986).

✔ Marital rape is an integral part of marital violence. Among women in San Francisco who had ever been married, 14% said they had been raped by a husband or ex-husband (I.H. Frieze & A. Browne, 1989).

✔ A Bureau of National Affairs report pegged the cost of domestic violence to U.S. companies at $3 to $5 *billion* annually from lost work time, increased health care costs, higher turnover rates, and lower productivity (The Boston Globe, March 11, 1992).

✔ Each year, domestic violence leads to 100,000 days of hospitalization, 30,000 emergency room visits, and almost 40,000 visits to a physician (American Medical Assoc., 1991).

✔ Almost one-fifth of all aggravated assaults reported to the police every week are reported by victims of assaults in the home. More than 21,000 domestic assaults, rapes and murders were reported to the police each week in 1991—twice the number of reported robberies (Majority Staff of the U.S. Senate Judiciary Committee, 1992).

✔ An Army survey. . . indicates that one out of every three families has suffered some kind of domestic violence, ranging from slapping and shoving to murder (Eric Schmidt, reprinted The Denver Post, May 23, 1994).

Effects of Domestic Violence on Children

✔ Children in a violent home learn that:
You hit people you love.
Males can be violent to females.
Parents hit children.
There is a moral rightness to use violence as a method of interaction.
When all else fails, use violence to get what you want.
Violence is a way to get rid of feelings, solve problems, and win.

✔ Children who witness or experience violence carry that experience with them into adulthood, at which time male children are much more likely to assault their partner and/or children than male children raised in a nonviolent household (U.S. Attorney General's Task Force on Family Violence, 1984).

The following information was adapted from data compiled by the Colorado Domestic Violence Coalition, National Center on Women and Family Law.

✔ Children and youth who witness abuse of their mothers display as much or more physical and verbal aggression, sleep disturbance, and general anxiety as those who are direct recipients of the abuse (Peter Jaffe, et al. *Journal of Orthopsychiatry*, 1986).

✔ Women who have been battered during pregnancy may begin to feel ambivalence or even hostility toward the unborn child because of her mistreatment and the mother-child bond can be hurt.

✔ Of the twenty-seven children murdered last year in New York who had been in protective care, 70% came from families that suffered from domestic violence (*New York Times*, 1992).

✔ Some children act out abusively at home and school using the behaviors they learned from their parents. Their anger is direct toward siblings, other children, animals, and adults (including their parents). They also may destroy property or vandalize.

✔ Children in violent or alcoholic homes are at risk for running away because they feel there is no hope for them at home.

✔ Children from abusive and violent homes may withdraw and be afraid to interact with other people from outside the home, or they may not know how to interact in a normal way.

✔ Children in violent homes can become self-destructive. They are at risk for suicide, depression, drug and alcohol abuse, teen pregnancy, eating disorders, careless driving, breaking the law, and problems with authority.

✔ Children from abusive homes are often unable to trust others or their world, or form reliable intimate relationships and have few friends.

✔ The self-esteem of children from abusive homes is destroyed and they distrust their own feelings.

✔ Developmental delays and regressions in children from violent homes are common in learning, verbal, and motor skills. They may have speech problems, learning disabilities, and school phobias.

✔ The children may have frequent headaches, skin diseases, insomnia, and other physical signs of emotionally induced disorders.

Violent Episodes

The purpose of the following exercise is to make you aware of how often and how deeply you have been influenced by violence in your personal life. Add as many pages as you need to cover each topic thoroughly.

Write a complete history of violent episodes where you were the perpetrator.

_____

_____

_____

Write a complete history of violent episodes where you were the victim.

_____

_____

_____

Write a complete history of violent episodes you were a witness to.

_____

_____

_____

Think about and describe the effects this violence has had on you.

_____

_____

_____

_____

Change is the Third Path
M. Lindsey, R. McBride and C. Platt

Where Am I Now?

Men usually enter therapy for two reasons. They have been arrested and are ordered into treatment by the court, or because of their violent or abusive behavior they are in danger of losing their relationship.

Most batterers entering therapy use and manipulate the therapeutic process. Believing that they will be able to "skate" through therapy without making changes, their goal is to use therapy as a tool to regain control of their lives—their wives, children and possessions. If you are like these men, you will be telling yourself that you will comply with therapy just enough to fulfill your "sentence" or to secure your mate's return.

Do you believe these things about your behavior?
>I did nothing wrong.
>I did something, but didn't think I would be caught.
>Even though I was caught, I can talk my way out of the problem.
>Although I got caught and couldn't talk my way out, I think the consequences will be light.

The process of therapy begins by looking at these four ideas. Do you hold these beliefs? Think about how you describe your violence. Whom do you blame? The victim? The police? The judge?

Have you read the definitions and the facts about domestic violence? If not, read them before going on. Then look at where you are right now.

>Remember—the exercises are not quizzes.
>There is no right or wrong, pass or fail, good or bad.
>The exercises will help you evaluate what is going on in your life.

You began your self-evaluation with *Violent Episodes* on page 10. Continue by completing the *What Went Wrong* exercise on the next page.

What Went Wrong?

What did I do wrong? _____
_____
_____

Why did I think I would not be caught?_____
_____
_____

How did I try to talk my way out of the problem
with the police? _____
with the judge? _____
with the probation officer? _____
with your partner? _____
with the therapist? _____

Did I beat the consequences?   ☐ Yes   ☐ No

How did I beat the consequences? _____
_____
_____

* * *

How Much Chaos?

Stability is the first step of recovery. The *Behavioral Checklist* will provide one method for identifying areas of your life that are out of control. Removing the chaos from your life can be frightening because you will have to start looking at your life—who you are and how you feel.

It may be difficult for you to answer the questions truthfully. However, you must be willing to answer the following questions honestly and confront each issue that is a problem for you with a long-range plan that is ethical and legal.

Ending your chaotic, violent, unethical, irresponsible, immoral, destructive and abusive behaviors will result in stability. From there, you can build a new life.

Change is the Third Path
M. Lindsey, R. McBride and C. Platt

Behavioral Checklist

Check all of the following that apply:

I was raised in a family with one or more of the following:

☐ Alcoholism/drugs   ☐ Violence   ☐ Mental health problems

☐ Parent loss   ☐ Child abuse   ☐ Frequent moves

I have had problems with:

☐ School work   ☐ School authorities   ☐ The law or police

☐ Work   ☐ Money   ☐ Other relationships

The following occurred in *past relationships*:

☐ Multiple relationships with women

☐ Separation(s)—how many?   ☐ Divorce(s)—how many?

☐ Restraining order issued   ☐ Partner's whereabouts unknown

☐ Partner left without warning   ☐ Custody battle

☐ Child visitation restricted   ☐ Children's whereabouts unknown

Check all of the following responses that apply to your behavior in any *past relationships*. Indicate the type of relationships involved.

☐ Poking   ☐ Pushing/Shoving   ☐ Grabbing

☐ Pulling hair   ☐ Restraining with hands   ☐ Restraining with objects

☐ Pinning to the ground, wall, or bed, etc.   ☐ Pushing to the ground

☐ Scratching/gouging (specify area of body)_____

☐ Kicking (specify area of body)_____

☐ Slapping with open hand (specify area of body)_____

☐ Punching with a closed fist (specify area of body)_____

☐ Biting (specify area of body)_____

☐ Choking   ☐ Choking to unconsciousness

☐ Attack partner with a knife, gun, or other weapon or object

☐ Other physical violence (specify)_____

_____

☐ Glaring at partner   ☐ Name calling/put-downs

☐ Blocking partner's path   ☐ Following /trailing your partner

☐ Spying/watching your partner

☐ Harassment outside the home (at partner's job, in public places etc.)

☐ Hinting or implying that violence against your partner is a possibility

☐ Control of partner's access to money

- ☐ Threats to take the children away   ☐ Threats to harm the children
- ☐ Threats to harm members of partner's family
- ☐ Threats to commit suicide if partner leaves
- ☐ Threats to leave or divorce partner
- ☐ Threats to have foreign born partner deported
- ☐ Withholding affection from partner   ☐ Withholding sex from partner
- ☐ Direct threats of violence/death
- ☐ Other psychological/emotional abuse (specify)_____

_____

- ☐ Grabbing sex organs or other body parts against partner's will.
- ☐ Forcing partner to perform unwanted sex acts
- ☐ Forcing partner to have sex with or in the presence of others, including children
- ☐ Forcing the use of objects during sex
- ☐ Forcing partner to view and/or imitate pornographic materials
- ☐ Forcing sexual intercourse on your partner
- ☐ Other sexual abuse (specify)_____

_____

- ☐ Punching walls, doors, etc.   ☐ Kicking walls, doors, etc.
- ☐ Breaking dishes, furniture, and/or other household items or personal objects
- ☐ Threatening to harm pets
- ☐ Other violence against property or pets (specify)_____

_____

Presently I have problems with chaos in the following areas:

- ☐ Job or school   ☐ Other relationships   ☐ Legal
- ☐ Alcohol or drugs   ☐ Other—explain_____

In my current relationship:

- ☐ I am separated.   ☐ My partner's whereabouts are unknown.
- ☐ I have been separated more than once.   ☐ My divorce is pending.
- ☐ A restraining order is issued against me.   ☐ I am involved in a custody battle.
- ☐ I am allowed no visitation with the children. ☐ My partner left without warning.
- ☐ I am looking for my partner.   ☐ I feel abandoned.
- ☐ I am unwilling to let go of my partner.
- ☐ I have difficulty concentrating, eating or sleeping because I am thinking about her.
- ☐ I blame my partner for my emotional injuries.
- ☐ I am hostile/angry/furious because I feel betrayed.

Change is the Third Path
M. Lindsey, R. McBride and C. Platt

☐ My relationship is extremely tense or volatile.

☐ I am extremely jealous and blame my partner for all types of promiscuous behavior.

☐ I have been violent before.

☐ I have attempted suicide.

☐ I continue to try to convince my partner she is wrong about the separation.

☐ I have access to a gun.

☐ I have used alcohol before, during or after fights with my partner.

☐ I use amphetamines, speed, cocaine, crack, or marijuana.

☐ I want to hurt my partner.

☐ I have no desire to stop my controlling or abusive or violent behavior.

Check all of the following responses that apply to your behavior in the relationship which resulted in your referral to this program.

Does this relationship involve a girlfriend____or wife____? If not, indicate the type of
relationship involved._____

☐ Poking	☐ Pushing/Shoving	☐ Grabbing
☐ Pulling hair	☐ Restraining with hands	☐ Restraining with objects
☐ Pinning to the ground, wall, or bed, etc.		☐ Pushing to the ground

☐ Scratching/gouging (specify area of body)_____

☐ Kicking (specify area of body)_____

☐ Slapping with open hand (specify area of body)_____

☐ Punching with a closed fist (specify area of body)_____

☐ Biting (specify area of body)_____

☐ Choking   ☐ Choking to unconsciousness

☐ Attack partner with a knife, gun, or other weapon or object

☐ Other physical violence (specify)_____

_____

☐ Glaring at partner	☐ Name calling/put-downs
☐ Blocking partner's path	☐ Following /trailing your partner

☐ Spying/watching your partner

☐ Harassment outside the home (At partner's job, in public places etc.)

☐ Hinting or implying that violence against your partner is a possibility

☐ Control of partner's access to money

☐ Threats to take the children away	☐ Threats to harm the children

☐ Threats to harm members of partner's family

- ☐ Threats to commit suicide if partner leaves
- ☐ Threats to leave or divorce partner
- ☐ Threats to have foreign born partner deported
- ☐ Withholding affection from partner   ☐ Withholding sex from partner
- ☐ Direct threats of violence/death
- ☐ Other psychological/emotional abuse (specify)_____
  _____

- ☐ Grabbing sex organs or other body parts against partner's will.
- ☐ Forcing partner to perform unwanted sex acts
- ☐ Forcing partner to have sex with or in the presence of others, including children.
- ☐ Forcing the use of objects during sex
- ☐ Forcing partner to view and/or imitate pornographic materials
- ☐ Forcing sexual intercourse on your partner
- ☐ Other sexual abuse (specify)_____
  _____

- ☐ Punching walls, doors, etc.   ☐ Kicking walls, doors, etc.
- ☐ Breaking dishes, furniture, and/or other household items or personal objects.
- ☐ Threatening to harm pets
- ☐ Other violence against property or pets (specify)_____
  _____

Crimes I have committed past or present:

☐ Harassment	☐ Disturbance	☐ Violating restraining order
☐ Menacing	☐ Assault	☐ Felony
☐ Drunk driving	☐ Selling drugs	☐ Embezzlement
☐ Robbery	☐ Burglary	☐ Rape ☐ Homicide

List other crimes_____

- ☐ Plea bargains in past related to domestic violence
- ☐ Arrests in past related to domestic violence
- ☐ Dismissed charge in past related to domestic violence

Take some time to evaluate your responses to the checklist.

Change is the Third Path
M. Lindsey, R. McBride and C. Platt

Batterers Who Stalk

A common feature of stalkers of individuals from past relationships is narcissistic injury (injury to your self interest). This injury can be real or perceived leaving the individual feeling "devastated," annihilated, betrayed, or abandoned. Stalkers often express the belief that everything for which they have worked has been stripped from them, creating a vast emptiness that is unbearable. These feelings are often accompanied by depression, anxiety, inability to sleep, work, eat or do day-to-day self care. Stalkers' problem solving ability is limited and they have a restricted sense of the future.

Individuals who stalk respond to this narcissistic injury by devising a "strategy" that they believe will heal the wound. This strategy always involves impacting on the "object"—the ex-significant other they believe is responsible for the pain. This object becomes the focus of their attempts to alleviate their narcissistic injury. They spend inordinate amounts of time, energy, and thought devising and implementing their plan. This process is closed and circular in nature in that these individuals grow increasingly isolated with irrational thoughts and intense feelings which act to support each other. The feelings intensify, reinforcing negative thoughts, until they act to create an absolute reality that is very difficult to alter.

Strategies

Three major strategies have been identified in batterers who stalk that produce abusive and destructive behavior. All stalking is not necessarily directed toward the goal of physically injuring the "object" of the obsession. In the case of reconciliation, the goal is regaining the lost object not hurting her. However, if the stalker fails in achieving this goal, the strategy could shift to another form.

Although physical injury is not the goal of reconciliation or vindication, there are always aspects of punishment in the form of fear inducement. In addition, while collecting information about the victim the perpetrator sometimes obtains information that "adds to his injury." This process can lead to explosive situations resulting in injury or death to many people.

Reconciliation

The goal of reconciliation is to get the person back and is a strategy that arises primarily from a feeling of abandonment, although loss of worth can play a role. When reconciliation is the goal, stalkers believe that they must have a specific person back or they will not survive. They are willing to do whatever is necessary to achieve this goal and are obsessive and compulsive in their efforts to accomplish it.

Getting their "object" back may involve seeking them, talking to them, therapy, making promises, involving family and friends to pressure the "object", and sending flowers and notes. It can also involve coercion, such as economic pressure, threats of force, threats to take the children, threats to kill, and suicidal behavior.

One stalker had taken a woman home twenty-two times at gun point. Contact with the woman confirmed her feelings of fear and terror. She would not file charges against the stalker because she knew he would kill her and/or her family. She did not believe anyone could protect her. She moved away with the stalker.

Many stalkers go to the woman's home or place of employment just "to talk" even when a restraining order exists. They believe that it is possible to persuade the victim to return. This tracking behavior is extremely abusive and dangerous. The individual being tracked feels terrorized by the constant violation of limits and boundaries. The danger to the victim is constant.

Vindication

Vindication is based on the goal of proving to "the world" that "I am good and she is bad." It includes an element of the need or desire for revenge in this strategy. "You hurt me and I will hurt you back." However, this is limited by the overriding motive to be seen by the "world" as the victim of the person they are stalking. The stalking is not just physical tracking behavior, but involves watching to collect information that can be used against the victim, collecting information from children and friends, calling Social Services, having custody evaluations, or using other court cases as avenues to attack the other person. They may write letters to family and friends that involve both attacks on character and recriminations about their victimization, as well as direct or veiled threats.

Revenge

Revenge is straightforward. Stalkers feel betrayed and annihilated. They believe this pain can be eliminated only through making the other person experience the same feeling. They may kill the "object" or their families. They often commit suicide along with the killing. These individuals feel justified in their behavior. The only method of controlling these individuals is jail.

Check all that apply in the following checklist. If you are engaged in stalking behavior, stop and get help immediately. Obsessive behavior is always potentially lethal.

Stalking Behavior Checklist

Tracking to Find Target

- [ ] Following
- [ ] Private investigator
- [ ] Mutual friends
- [ ] Family of the target
- [ ] Family of the stalker
- [ ] Employers
- [ ] Department of Motor Vehicles
- [ ] Post office
- [ ] Children
- [ ] Social services
- [ ] Custody battles
- [ ] Telephones and telephone company
- [ ] Cruising
- [ ] Pizza delivery

Information Gathering When Stalker Knows Location of Target

- [ ] Following
- [ ] Private investigator
- [ ] Mutual friends
- [ ] Family of the target
- [ ] Family of the stalker
- [ ] Employers
- [ ] Department of Motor Vehicles
- [ ] Post Office
- [ ] Children
- [ ] Social services
- [ ] Custody battles
- [ ] Telephone interrogation
- [ ] Sitting outside of home
- [ ] Going to where she will be
- [ ] Peeping
- [ ] Eaves-dropping
- [ ] Medical records
- [ ] Checking ash trays and trash
- [ ] Checking victim's purse
- [ ] Reading victim's journals
- [ ] Reading victim's check register
- [ ] Lawsuits, deposition

Domestic Violence: Crimes Committed on Victim While Separated

- [ ] Violation of restraining order
- [ ] Threats of death, physical harm, bombing
- [ ] Harassment
- [ ] Burglary
- [ ] Criminal trespass
- [ ] Destruction of property
- [ ] Violation of no contact order
- [ ] Disturbing peace or disorderly conduct
- [ ] Assault or battery
- [ ] Arson
- [ ] Theft

Terrorist Activities or Punishment

- [ ] Leaving objects, such as wood chips, feces, prizes; object tied to car; love notes; or hate mail
- [ ] Attempts to destroy reputation: letters, fliers, dissemination of private information, distortion of truth or facts
- [ ] False or misleading reports to authorities
- [ ] Killing or stealing pets
- [ ] Drive-bys
- [ ] Destruction of property
- [ ] Watching or following
- [ ] Tying up telephone or fax lines
- [ ] Symbolic messages

Behaviors Specific to Stalkers While in the Relationship

- [ ] Interrogation of victim
- [ ] Checking all drawers in home for evidence
- [ ] Checking mileage
- [ ] Timing victim's activities
- [ ] Peeping
- [ ] Eaves-dropping
- [ ] Putting something in or on the home so he can know if she comes or goes
- [ ] Interrogation of children
- [ ] Checking ash trays and trash
- [ ] Checking victim's purse
- [ ] Reading victim's journals
- [ ] Reading victim's check register
- [ ] Medical records

Stalking Behavior Present: [ ] Yes   [ ] No

What Do I Think?

Accountability for choices is the cornerstone of recovery. Violence is always a choice, not an automatic response to provocation. *Provocation* is a concept that encourages individuals to blame others for their choice to be violent.

Conflict exists in all relationships. The source of conflict can be another person's behavior and violence is one method of resolving the conflict. The source of the violence lies within the individual and is not the result of external pressures, provocations, issues, demands, stressors or the actions of others. Accepting responsibility for using violence as a response to conflict is absolutely necessary if you are going to stop your abusive and violent behavior. Answer the following questions.

How should violence in the family be handled? _____

_____

Is family violence a crime? ☐ Yes ☐ No

Why? _____

_____

Who was at fault for the violence in my situation and why? _____

_____

Review the *Behavioral* and *Stalking Behavior Checklist* then answer the following questions.

Have I committed any crimes? ☐ Yes ☐ No

How many crimes have I committed?_____

How many crimes have I committed that I was never arrested for?

_____

Were my consequences less or more than I deserved? _____

Am I full of anger and resentment because I am being unjustly punished or because I feel ashamed and afraid? _____

How I Looked at the Violent Incident When it Occurred

Many people think or act as thought their behavior is in direct response to external forces. In fact, our behavior is organized by internal forces such as attitudes, values, beliefs or rules.

Your actions are always preceded by feelings and thoughts. When you are abusive and violent, to say, "It just happened" is not the truth. You made a choice to act the way you did. This exercise is designed to help you examine your internal dialogue as it relates to the violent episode. Think back to the event then describe your feelings and thoughts.

The Event

↓

My Feelings and Thoughts

↓

My Behavior

What were my feelings just prior to the violence? _____
_____
_____

How did they promote violence? _____
_____
_____

What were my thoughts just prior to the violence? _____
_____
_____

How did they promote violence? _____
_____
_____

How did I explain the violence to others? _____
_____
_____

How did my explanation of the incident justify my violence? _____
_____
_____

The Cost of My Violent Behavior

The choice to use abusive and violent behavior to resolve conflict has consequences. The worksheet divides the results of your violence into consequences you have received and those the other person has received. List all the consequences you can think of.

As you list the damage you have done to others, ask yourself if you care about them. Examine your attitude. Do you think they "deserved" what they got?

Do you feel "all right" about some of their pain but not all of it? People who are assaultive often believe that it is okay to hurt those who have hurt them.

Consequences to Myself

Internal
Shame (examples)

_____

_____

_____

_____

_____

External
Debt

_____

_____

_____

_____

_____

Consequences to Others

Internal
Emotional injuries

_____

_____

_____

_____

_____

_____

External
Bruises

_____

_____

_____

_____

_____

_____

If you are willing to continue to pay the consequences associated with your violent and abusive behavior, then put this book away until you are ready to make a change in your life.

If you are willing to alter your behavior, keep reading.

Change is the Third Path
M. Lindsey, R. McBride and C. Platt

Stability and Chaos

When life has become unmanageable *it is not an accident.* Problems such as alcohol and drug abuse, legal or economic difficulties are often the result of poor choices. You probably have many problems besides your abusive and violent behavior. You may appear calm and well-ordered to the outside world while your internal world is a disordered confusion of activities and feelings. You have good moments when you feel successful, loved and connected. Yet, the feelings that good times cannot last long or that you really do not belong persist. Thus, it's always easier to be on your way somewhere else—another job, town, woman, or project—than it is to maintain what you have already accomplished.

When you let the level of stimulation drop, you feel what is really inside, so you avoid your internal world as much as you can, ignoring the wreckage you have left behind. Surviving the emptiness requires having something to focus on, anything to fill the void. When you decide what is needed in order to "feel good," you may become obsessive and pursue this course with great energy. Your obsession may be sex, work, sports, drugs, alcohol, or a fantasy world. Stimulation and chaos often replace any real human contact. They temporarily patch the empty hole you feel inside and help displace the sense of failure you may feel over being unsuccessful at work, ill at ease with your mate and family or desperately unhappy.

If your obsession is a woman, things will go well until your internal demand to reduce the pain eventually exceeds the ability of the relationship to alleviate the pain.

The only way to resolve your internal conflict and heal your pain is by stabilizing your life. Without stability, no long-term change is possible. The cost of stability is frighteningly high to abusive and violent men: giving up the use of illegal drugs, getting treatment for alcohol and drug abuse, giving up affairs and gambling, cleaning up all your legal and financial problems, going to work, and most importantly, giving up abusive and violent behavior. You also need to give up other forms of chaos such as working excessively, addictively seducing women, and breaking promises, but these may take a longer period of time.

The worksheets that you have completed in this section and the one that follows, titled Chaos, will help you begin to identify the chaos in your life. Chaos is like an avalanche chasing you down a hill. The more chaos you create, the bigger the avalanche and the steeper the hill. Eventually you will get run over. Fill in the blanks and then be prepared to seek help for each area you identify.

If you stop creating chaos, the avalanche will lose its momentum and you will leave it behind. Stability is a choice that you must make every day. You face three outcomes to the process of stabilization: you can continue to live in chaos, you can die, or you can change. The third path is the most frightening.

Chaos

List behaviors that create chaos in your life.

_____

_____

_____

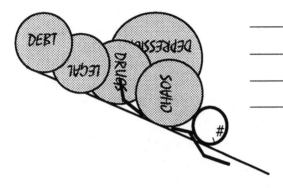

List possible solutions for stopping the chaos.

_____

_____

_____

_____

When can I leave my chaotic behavior behind?

_____

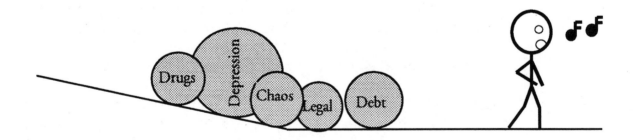

If you do not have a solution, take the issue to your therapist or group for feedback.

Change is the Third Path
M. Lindsey, R. McBride and C. Platt

The Role of Alcohol and Drugs in Violence

There are three aspects of every violent act.

The perpetrator must have access to the victim.

There has to be impetus in the form of internal or external conflict.

The perpetrator loses the inhibitions that normally restrain aggression.

In addition for a man to act violently he must have "permission" either from himself or from society at large. Our society gives soldiers and police permission to be violent in designated circumstances. Certain religions give their agents permission to use violence against unbelievers or those who break their rules. Some parents claim Biblical injunction or family tradition as permission to use violence against their children. Similarly battering men feel entitled to use violence against mates who violate their "rules."

Drugs especially alcohol act as powerful mechanisms to reduce intellectual control over our emotions. When the ethics, morals, beliefs, or rules that guide us are suppressed there is a much greater chance that we will act on impulses based on raw emotions.

If you are going to stop being abusive and violent, it is imperative that you do everything possible to increase inhibitions against the use of force. This means eliminating all forms of disinhibition, such as, alcohol and drugs, victim blaming, dehumanization of people, peer support for violence, modeling for violence in sports, movies, and television shows.

The best method for increasing inhibitors is consequences. Intervention with a perpetrator requires strengthening inhibitors against violence through arrest, criminal prosecution, conviction, probation, and offender-specific therapy. No abusive and violent man wants to look deeply and honestly at his life. There is fear, shame, guilt, powerlessness, worthlessness, and humiliation. These feelings can combine with a powerful need for control that can lead you to generate a specific strategy to resist external limits placed on your behavior.

Ultimately if your abuse and violence is going to stop, you must internalize a new set of values and skills that act as inhibitors against violence. This process of internal and external constraint can evaporate when alcohol and drugs are present. Alcohol and drug use by men who are abusive and violent represents an extreme danger. Experience shows that people with a history of explosive or abusive behavior should not use alcohol or drugs.

Take an inventory of your substance usage.
Note: Substance means any drug of choice you use. Alcohol is a drug.

1. What are your substances of choice? 1 for first choice, 2 for second choice and so on.

I do not use any substances. ☐
Alcohol: Beer_____Wine_____Vodka_____Gin_____
            Whiskey_____Scotch_____Mix drinks_____Other_____
Marijuana (THC)_____   Hashish_____
Uppers_____   Downers_____
Cocaine (specify)_____   LSD_____
Morphine_____   Heroin_____
Other (specify)_____

2. Do you feel that any of these substances have ever been a problem to you?   ☐ Yes   ☐ No

3. Does your family feel you use substances too much?
                                        ☐ Yes   ☐ No

4. How old were you when you started any of these substances? _____years old

5. What substance did you first start using?_____

6. Do you ever use a substance(s) until you pass out?
                                        ☐ Yes   ☐ No

7. Have you ever had a blackout?   ☐ Yes   ☐ No
              If yes, how often?_____

8. Do you get angry when someone tells you about your using?
                                        ☐ Yes   ☐ No

Change is the Third Path
M. Lindsey, R. McBride and C. Platt

9. How often do you use? (Check as they apply)

    a. Substance

☐ Less than once a week   ☐ Once a week   ☐ Several times a week
☐ Weekends   ☐ Daily   ☐ Binge(sporadic, intense usage)
☐ Other (specify)_____

    b. Substance

☐ Less than once a week   ☐ Once a week   ☐ Several times a week
☐ Weekends   ☐ Daily   ☐ Binge(sporadic, intense usage)
☐ Other (specify)_____

    c. Substance

☐ Less than once a week   ☐ Once a week   ☐ Several times a week
☐ Weekends   ☐ Daily   ☐ Binge(sporadic, intense usage)
Other (specify)_____

10. Have you used a substance daily in the past two months?
        ☐ Yes   ☐ No

11. Do you use substances during your work day?
        ☐ Yes   ☐ No

12. Can you stop using without a struggle at any time?
        ☐ Yes   ☐ No

13. Do friends or relatives think you use substances more or less than other people who use?
    ☐ less   ☐ same   ☐ more

14. Has your substance usage caused you to lose a job?
        ☐ Yes   ☐ No

15. Have you gotten into trouble at work because of substance use?
        ☐ Yes   ☐ No

16. Have you ever neglected your obligations, your family or your work for two or more days in a row because you were using substances?
        ☐ Yes   ☐ No

17. Have you awakened the morning after some substance usage the night before and found that you could not remember part of the evening before?   ☐ Yes   ☐ No

18. Do you need to use substances the "morning after" to get rid of a "hangover"?   ☐ Yes   ☐ No

19. Have you ever attended a meeting of Alcoholics Anonymous (AA) or Narcotics Anonymous (NA) other than as a guest?   ☐ Yes   ☐ No

20. Have you ever passed out in the past year due to excessive usage?   ☐ Yes   ☐ No

21. Have you ever been told that you have liver trouble or cirrhosis?   ☐ Yes   ☐ No

22. Have you had delirium tremens (D.T.'s) sever shaking, heard voices, or seen things that weren't there after heavy drinking ?   ☐ Yes   ☐ No

23. Have you ever been arrested, even for a few hours because of intoxicated behavior?   ☐ Yes   ☐ No

24. Have you been charged with any drunken or under the influence driving offenses in the past six months?   ☐ Yes   ☐ No

25. Do you ever feel bad about your substance usage?   ☐ Yes   ☐ No

26. Has your substance usage ever created problems between you and your significant other or wife?   ☐ Yes   ☐ No

27. Has your significant other or wife (or other family member) ever gone to anyone for help about your substance usage?   ☐ Yes   ☐ No

What we said in the beginning of this book needs repeating here. If there is any chance for you to make positive changes in your life and develop a new and constructive set of values and skills, you will need to surrender to and accept the idea that your life is unmanageable and you are powerless to make the necessary changes without outside help. You must give up your agenda and begin to accept outside feedback and control.

Change is the Third Path
M. Lindsey, R. McBride and C. Platt

Male Gender Training

Thirty years later and nothing has changed. The events of the playground are timeless as I strove to master its vagaries, to try and control the people and places around me. I've been beaten by bullies, caught up in exciting crowds as they passed by, leaving me reeling in the soft sand.
David Garton, *The Playground.* 1990

Violence is a male problem

According to United States Department of Justice statistics—*Uniform Crime Report 1992: Table 37–Total Arrest Trends, Sex, 1991-1992.*

87.4 % of those arrested for all violent crimes were men.

90.5 % of those arrested for murder were men.

98.7 % of forcible rapes were committed by men.

91.5 % of robberies were committed by men.

85.2 % of those arrested for aggravated assaults were men.

92.3 % of those arrested for sex offenses (not rape or prostitution) were men.

82.0 % of those arrested for offenses against family and children were men.

Wars are instigated and carried out by men.

Training to be a man equals training to be violent

Virtually every man has experienced violence in his life and is trained to use violence for resolving conflict if he deems it necessary. Most men have engaged in fist fights, verbal threats, pushing, shoving, grabbing, or intimidation. For almost all men, the use of physical force to resolve conflict is an option that they have experienced in at least one of three ways: they have used physical force to win; they have been victims of physical force; or they have seen others use physical force. Violence for men is a common experience and under many circumstances some men view violence as an acceptable response to a threat from either men or women. The threat need not be physical harm; it could be a threat to self-worth. Acknowledging violence as normal male behavior is important for the understanding of domestic violence.

Two reasons for male violence

The process of molding violent men begins very early and is a pattern of development our society considers normal. First, almost all societies want men to have the potential to use physical force as a legitimate means to resolve conflict. Societies sanction violence in specific circumstances such as war, police activities, defense of self and family, and sports. Historically men have trained to wage war in order to protect family, clan, city or state or to expand the domain that each family, clan, city or state controls. Whether it is used for protection or expansion, violence helps ensure the survival of the culture for which men fight. And for thousands of years, men have been willing to risk death or dismemberment to protect their cultures. Several conditions enable men to go to war and kill or be killed (*The Training* below will describe these conditions). Training for violence starts within the family and with the games of childhood.

The second reason for male violence is that many men have been given neither the means to determine acceptable boundaries for violence nor have they been given the tools to resolve conflict without resorting to coercion. Many men come from families that injure rather than protect. These men are left with a pervasive sense of alienation, loneliness, inadequacy, mistrust, and fear, and they have no adequate means of coping with these feelings.

Men who were abused as children, i.e. were victims of violence inflicted by their families, are unable to establish acceptable personal boundaries for themselves or others and frequently feel threats to their self-worth as threats to their survival. When abusive men perceive themselves as threatened, hence endangered by emotional conflict, they do all they can to win and survive. If they cannot assure emotional survival by lesser means, they will use violence.

The training

Men develop the following personality characteristics as part of male sex-role training.

Sense of right

Engendered in males is the idea that they may hurt or kill to enforce justice, right wrongs and punish. A man is taught that he is doing what is necessary and correct when he hurts those who "deserve" it.

You may perceive your mate's behavior as immoral, unfair or inadequate. When an abusive and violent man believes that his mate has hurt him in some fashion, he feels he is within his rights to injure her.

Sense of duty

Men who go to war know they may die. They risk death because they have been taught that death is preferable to being thought cowardly. Men have been taught that it is their duty to defend their families or culture from danger. Some men feel overwhelmed by this responsibility and run away from the family, while others remain and are resentful.

Change is the Third Path
M. Lindsey, R. McBride and C. Platt

Even though you may resent your feelings of duty to your mate, you may not be able to leave her because of your guilt over disobeying what you perceives as a cultural imperative. You may alternate between stability and instability, responsibility and irresponsibility, reason and rage. Your erratic feelings have little, if anything, to do with your mate's behavior. They reflect your internal sense or belief about your ability to be the man you think you should be. You probably doubt your ability to be the protector, guide, teacher or leader of your family, and this failure is too great to bear. As a result you blame, attack and criticize others or retreat into alcohol, drugs, sex or work.

Ability to objectify	In war, men do not kill people; instead, they kill objects. These objects are Gooks, Krauts, Japs, Yanks, Communists, Imperialists. The list is long and as old as mankind. The process of objectifying is critical to the process of killing.

In your relationship you may hit, injure or kill a "bitch," "whore," or "slut." She ceases to be a loved one. She is only an object.

Sense of disconnection	Men are not as connected to other people as women are. They are trained to be impersonal and distant. It is hard enough to risk death without having to face a massive loss of joy and closeness. Men are taught to substitute ideology for connection or to put ideology before connection to people.

As with many other men who are abusive, you may have been abused and your self-worth is very low. You are less in touch with your feelings than most men. You have walled off your internal world because it was too painful and confusing for you as a child. You may be struggling to survive and to prevent yourself from being destroyed. You have been betrayed and no matter how great your desire, you cannot afford to risk becoming close to others. The loss of someone close would only serve to further alienate you from other people. As an abusive man, you rely on traditional male ideology because you lack an understanding of how it separates you from authentic personal feelings. You probably believe that expressing emotion and asking for help shows weakness and leaves you vulnerable to attack.

Goal directedness	Men are trained to take charge and find solutions to problems. Once the abusive man perceives he is injured, he falls back on the rules he has learned about hierarchy and action. If something is causing pain, you believe you must take charge to stop the pain. If you perceive that "something" to be your mate, then you move to stop her behavior.
Ideology is more important than people.	Men are trained to believe that ideology is more important than individual human life. At first glance, this seems either untrue or a belief limited to fanatics. Yet our society tolerates conditions which condemn children to malnutrition, young men and women to decaying, crime-ridden neighborhoods, and millions of adults to joblessness because of economic

ideology. Societies, religions and political groups all rest on ideological positions for which men are assumed to be willing to fight.

Male sex role training, the expression of the ideology of male authority and domination, gives men permission to control other people. The concept that one person is entitled to dominate another is the ideology prevalent in abusive relationships.

Might equals right

Strength and physical force can determine who is going to survive, who will get status and power. To be on the losing side of a conflict is to risk losing everything. Men are taught that violence is a useful method for resolving conflict, for achieving status and power, for surviving. Some come to believe their survival and winning depends on violence.

In a battering relationship, unless the woman uses a weapon, the man will almost always win. In general men are bigger, stronger and better trained to fight. Even if the abusive man seldom hits, once he intimidates the victim, he can control her behavior.

The abusive man expands the boundaries of violence beyond sanctioned limits. You wrongly assume the authority to use violence in situations where you feel threatened or humiliated. As with all abusive and violent men, you justify your violence because you believe conflict is dangerous and you do not know how to resolve conflict peacefully.

Violence is not okay on any level—personal, national, or international.

What it Means to be Male

Men who are interested in recovery and change will need to struggle with the concept of what it means to be male. You can begin by answering the following questions. The answers will give you the beginning point for a discussion in group which in turn could bring you closer to understanding the meaning of being male.

What did my father teach me about what it means to be a man?_____
_____
_____

What did my mother teach me about what it means to be a man? _____
_____
_____

What did my peers teach me about what it means to be a man? _____
_____

What did the movies and television teach me about what it means to be a man?_____
_____

Who were my heroes and why were they my heroes? _____
_____
_____

How do I act with men? _____
_____

How do I act with women?_____
_____

Why do I act one way when I am with men and another when I am with women? _____
_____

Masculine and Feminine Traits

Men and women hold beliefs about how the opposite sex should behave. These beliefs create expectations which are fertile grounds for conflict. When we decide what is correct or acceptable behavior for others, we risk exerting control in an attempt to dominate.

To achieve equality in your relationships, it will be necessary to examine your views, beliefs, attitudes and expectations of the opposite sex. Go over this exercise with your mate or female friends. Their input will help you understand women.

Challenging your views of women can help you establish a new set of behaviors which may help you have more productive and meaningful interactions.

List all the traits necessary to be a man.

_____
_____
_____
_____
_____
_____

List all the traits necessary to be a woman.

_____
_____
_____
_____
_____
_____

List all the traits necessary to be a complete human being.

_____
_____
_____
_____
_____
_____

Change is the Third Path
M. Lindsey, R. McBride and C. Platt

Characteristics of Batterers

This chapter is a compilation of what clinical experience has shown us about batterers. The diversity of descriptions supports our view that these men have a variety of dysfunctional attitudes, behaviors and resulting dynamics and may in fact have personality disorders.

Since most men are socialized to believe that violence is an option for resolving some conflicts, this training, combined with childhood abuse and neglect, makes their use of violence in intimate relationships more likely. Many men choose to react with violence when they are hurt, frightened, threatened, attacked, feeling guilty, failing or feeling any other ego-threatening emotion. For batterers the choice to use violence as a means for resolving conflict is made based on the following beliefs:

> The world is a dangerous place.
> I must survive.
> I can trust only myself.
> I will get what I want when I want it.
> I'm doing nothing wrong.
> I won't get caught.
> If I get caught, I can talk my way out of the situation.
> If I can't get out of it, the consequences will be light.

The batterer uses violence for a number of reasons: he wants his mate to stop a specific behavior, he wants her to do something differently, or he wants to punish her, but few violent men will acknowledge that such behavior is abusive.

To the violent man battering is always what other men do or it is always a behavior that is more severe than anything the batterer has done. The abusive man believes batterers are somebody else—they are crazy people who cannot control their tempers or unhappy drunks who beat their mates for no reason, but he's not one of them. He doubts the truth that his behavior is intimidating or controlling. He believes that his threat or use of force is necessary to handle the situation or to stop his emotional pain. He feels responsible for his mate and family as "master of his home," and thinks this sense of responsibility justifies his behavior.

Minimizing his behavior, the abusive man does not see it as unusual or extreme. The rationale that follows is typical: If he shouted his mate into submission, he defines abuse as slapping. Although he choked her, he describes the incident as "holding her by the shoulders." If he held her down, he calls it restraining her because she was out of control. If he hit her, he insists it wasn't very hard or "not like hitting a man." He reasons that it was her fault because if she had not provoked him, he would never have beaten her.

Because the man is damaged emotionally from his experiences in childhood, he continuously builds emotional walls to control the world, to protect his fragile self, and to keep away what he desperately needs and desires most in life—safety, closeness, and friendship. The paradox is that the traits which he has developed to protect himself from pain and to create satisfaction are the barriers which now cause pain and keep him from attaining satisfaction. If someone, usually his mate, gets around the walls he feels threatened. He acts as if his survival is in danger and strikes out.

While the severity, depth, and complexity of their problems and violence vary greatly, men who batter share many common life experiences and characteristics (see the Abusive and Violent Man model on the next page). However, the manifestation of these characteristics is complex. Clearly, abusive and violent men are not identical. They do not fit a stereotypical description, but have a number of the following characteristics in greater or lesser degree.

Excessive need for control

We all need to be able to exercise control over our lives. We need to influence, direct, or regulate people and activities that affect us. It is healthy to establish reasonable boundaries or limits for ourselves and to be assertive. In the process, we also learn to respect other people's boundaries.

At some point in our lives, all of us have used unhealthy methods of gaining control: avoidance of conflict, passive-aggressive behavior, unresponsiveness, appeasing, placating, or threats of violence.

The difference between the abusive man and other men is that he has carried controlling to an extreme. He has an excessive need to gain and maintain control not only over his life but over the lives of others. His goal becomes control of every aspect of life whether it is his wife's manner of dress or the speed at which traffic moves. Since this level of control is impossible to attain, he is frustrated and engaged in exhausting conflict all of the time. The use of psychological or physical violence as a means of gaining and maintaining control over his relationships is the universal trait of the abusive and violent man.

Abusive and Violent Men

Childhood Trauma

Physical abuse

Sexual abuse

Emotional abuse

Neglect

Abandonment

Male Gender Training

Sense of right
Sense of duty
Ability to objectify
Emotionally disconnected
Goal directed
Ideology more important than people
Might equals right

Form Belief System

The world is a dangerous place
I will survive
I can trust only myself
I will get what I want when I want it
I'm doing nothing wrong
I won't get caught
If I get caught, I can talk my walk out of the situation
If I can't get out of it, the consequences will be light

Characteristics

Controlling
Lacks assertiveness skills
Undependable or over-responsible
Over-stimulated and chaotic
Fearful of abandonment
Unable to handle criticism

Socially isolated
Masked by facade
Misogynistic
Holds irrational beliefs
Alienated
Obsessive
Low self-esteem

The abusive man has an inordinate need to control because his life in childhood felt out of his control. He came from a home in which, as a child, he could never win. The rules were unfair, rigid, inconsistent, or unclear. As a child he may at first have struggled to make sense of the rules and to please his parents. Eventually, however, he stopped struggling to please and in anger and despair, found ways to gain control of his life through acting out, lying, avoidance or depression. Rejecting his parents' disorganization, pathology or their physical or emotional coercion, the boy rejected both parental authority and by extension, outside feedback and control.

A child's rejection of parental control has far-reaching implications and effects. Children who cannot make sense of the information coming from their parents have no reason to believe that information from the world outside the family can be trusted or makes sense. Therefore, any outside feedback, influence or control is suspect. The violent man-to-be interprets outside influence or feedback as criticism and "noise." In order to survive and develop his identity the child decides that since nobody in his family is responding adequately to his needs, he must insure those needs are met by doing for himself and trusting only himself.

The motivation to control also varies greatly among violent men according to differences in personality and relationships. One man may be desperately trying to keep his wife from leaving; another man may want his mate out of the way. A man may want to control his wife either because she is doing something he dislikes or because she is not doing something he wants. However, the basic need that motivates the man to control is the same as it was when he was a child: to make his world as safe and predictable as possible.

The reasons men give for battering their mates are many. But no matter what the given reason, the fact is that the abusive man batters his mate in an effort to maintain control. That is, the man who batters does so when his feelings and life are out of control. He has very strong emotions and no method of coping. All he knows is that what he is experiencing feels life-threatening and that he must make the threat end. Since the batterer believes that the source of his pain and discomfort is external—his mate—he becomes determined to force her to change her behavior.

People who do not understand male violence assume that a woman who is battered has done something to provoke—therefore to deserve—the beating she has gotten. Her behavior may have angered her batterer, but frequently what provokes the batterer comes entirely from his skewed perceptions or projections or fears of what other people think/expect of him. A few examples reported by men in therapy groups are as follows:

Change is the Third Path
M. Lindsey, R. McBride and C. Platt

A man held a gun to his wife's head because the mileage in the car was off by two-tenths of a mile. He thought this meant she had taken a detour to have an affair.

A man broke his spouse's jaw because the butter was not unwrapped. He was angry because this indicated she was disrespectful of him.

A man beat his wife because two men whistled at her. He believed the harassment was her fault because she was wearing a short skirt.

A man battered his mate because her nephews ruined a picnic. He claimed she was responsible because they were part of her family.

The man who batters tries to avoid loss of control at all cost. He must be on guard to protect himself not only from physical harm but more importantly from emotional harm. He is extremely sensitive to challenges, embarrassment, and failures. He fears that his worldly possessions, those things that he struggled so hard to obtain—job, money, home or mate—could be taken away. It would diminish him to lose the things that were suppose to give him happiness and satisfaction.

He jumps from situation to situation in an effort to maximize control over his life. However, he doesn't realize the paradox. The more he tries to control, the less control he has. He becomes exhausted and confused. He continues to lose the little ability he has to control his life and in the end destroys everything he values. As his fear and pain increase, he begins to justify striking out in rage in an effort to eliminate these feelings. Violence ensues when lesser forms of control fail.

Isolation from society

Since human beings are social creatures, most of us like living in an interactive community. We feel safe and are challenged, stimulated, and entertained by other people. There is no denying that living together has its problems, but ordinarily most people are able to work these out reasonably.

However, some people try to separate or set themselves apart. They want to be free of external influences. They want to insulate themselves from the demands of society, are afraid of relationships and do not trust others. One mechanism to limit control by others is isolation. The batterer finds it safer to isolate himself and his family. If he is not around other people, he reasons, they will have no power over him.

In part, isolation is an artifact of the need for control. Because the batterer was deeply injured as a child, he needs to protect himself from the possible pain of dealing with people. Isolation protects him from experiencing rejection, humiliation, domination or challenges to his belief system. He irrationally sees the world as threatening, unreliable, and likely to take advantage of or hurt him because he sees himself as weak and vulnerable.

Rather than viewing other people as sources of help or support, the abusive man considers them dangerous.

The need or desire for isolation has its roots in many places. Some men lack the skills needed to interact reasonably with people—small talk, responsiveness, basic social skills. Other men stay separate in order to limit other people's ability to place demands upon them. If there are a limited number of demands on the batterer, he can have more time to do what he wants. Even if the battering man wants to have more friends and engage in a wide range of activities, he find himself overwhelmed and in conflict with the demands placed upon him by his family. His easiest resolution is to eliminate the outside source of contact, information, or support. This pattern continues to repeat and intensify.

Isolation also arises for these men from a sense of alienation. The man who batters perceives himself as never having fit in with the rest of society. Somehow, he sees himself as separate from and unlike all others. He may have given up on the idea that he will ever be accepted by other people. He may feel that other people can "go to hell" if they question his behavior or he may constantly struggle to have relationships with neighbors, co-workers, or family. In attempting to do so, his controlling behavior, lack of well-defined boundaries, and inability to control his temper usually lead to problems in these endeavors. For example, he will allow others to cross his boundaries inappropriately and then explode when he has had enough. He will often get angry, yell, and threaten. He may then walk away from the conflict and terminate the relationship rather than endure the guilt, embarrassment, or humiliation he feels at not fitting in. He usually has no negotiation skills available to mediate the conflict. Consequently he has little social life, a few casual buddies but no real male friends. His world usually becomes limited to his mate, a job, and a few activities.

Finally, isolation can be the result of the chaos in the violent relationship. His low self-esteem may overwhelm him with the fear of losing his mate. He might struggle to build her a castle or prison in which he can keep her. The obsession with the struggle in the relationship takes his energy, time, and money. His obsessive fear of losing his mate consumes his energy, time and money and only serves to increase his isolation thus escalating his fear of loss so it continues on and on. The greater the struggle, the greater the expenditure of these resources. The more the man and woman need each other, the more intense the struggle and the greater the potential for isolation.

Lack of assertiveness skills

Being assertive is asking directly for what you want or need and refusing directly what you don't want or need. Assertive people consider both their rights and the rights of others when faced with conflict in communicating, decision-making, and problem-solving. Passive people tend to consider only the rights of others while aggressive people tend to consider only their rights.

Change is the Third Path
M. Lindsey, R. McBride and C. Platt

Men who batter have trouble being assertive. This lack of assertiveness arises from two sources, a feeling of entitlement and a feeling of unworthiness. Oddly, the man who enters treatment for violence often has a very difficult time asking for what he wants. He fears rejection or disappointment. He attempts to get his needs met by indirectly hinting, by over-giving, or by hoping or assuming that somehow his mate will or should "know" what he needs. He may simply decide that what he wants "will be" despite the consequences to his mate or children.

Generally, the abusive man will avoid conflict because it frightens him and because he lacks sufficient skills to deal with it. But he cannot avoid the frustrations of everyday life. Tension and anxiety continually build in him. Typically, he lets things build up and then explodes. These may be mini-explosions such as yelling, honking his car horn, "flipping off" other drivers, or cussing at traffic delays. These little bursts of anger neither alleviate his angry, resentful feelings nor build his sense of mastery in communications, decision-making, or problem-solving. These bursts of anger serve to increase the likelihood of a greater explosion because they achieve short-term success but create long-term problems. Furthermore these violent episodes often pass without any consequences. Inevitably, when he is overwhelmed and perceives few consequences, he will release his emotional pain in an explosion during a conflict with his partner.

Abusive and violent men vacillate between passivity and aggression. For example, one man convinced himself that he could create a sanctuary where his wife could grow and heal from the pain of her life. She flirted with men, used drugs, and almost sent him into bankruptcy with her spending sprees. However, he was unable to say no to her because he was afraid she would leave him. He was too frightened to set limits and tell her he could not live in that way, so he created an illusion: "If I take care of her, she will change and then I can get what I need."

A second man was so afraid his wife would be seduced by another man that he demanded she not leave the house without him. He made sure all the doors and windows were sealed with tape when he left the house. He checked the tape on his return to see if the seals were broken. Since neither over-giving nor controlling provided relief from the men's unending fears, both strategies failed and violence ensued.

An abusive man can be a passive man who cannot say no or a man who is so threatened and insecure that he says no all of the time in an attempt to control everything. Few men who are reasonably assertive about what they want and need and are secure in themselves batter their mates.

Well-developed facade

All people have weaknesses or characteristics that they are afraid to show the world. From time to time, most people try to hide or minimize real or perceived failures or personal deficits to avoid discomfort. But all batterers live behind a facade.

For some the facade may be only the social lie that covers their abusiveness toward their wives, girlfriends and children. The man who assaults his wife or girlfriend does not disclose his battering behavior and until a crisis occurs, neither does she. For many reasons: shame, fear, feelings of powerlessness, hope that the batterer will change—his victim may cover for him, denying or minimizing his violence. Children in the family collaborate in maintaining the social front that all is normal in their home. Most children feel powerless to change the family situation and when they try to intervene, they may be punished or be injured during the violent episodes.

Friends of the batterer may observe his verbal or even his physical abuse and choose not to comment. If they care about the man or his family, they may want to view his abusiveness as atypical, a one-time event. If his behavior does not correspond to their overall impression of his character, they will dismiss it, thus allowing the batterer's social facade to stay in place.

Because at the professional and managerial levels society tolerates verbal abusiveness in the service of high levels of performance and terms "successful" the man who earns a high income, people may not consider that the verbally abusive professional or manager is abusive in his intimate relationships as well, because his status puts his behavior beyond scrutiny.

The social facade under which the batterer hides is harmful, but even more harmful is the facade of another kind which a batterer may develop to hide his real goals, agendas, fantasies and behavior. This level of facade is nearly impenetrable. Only the most acute therapist will detect it, and even then only after months of working with the man.

The process of building a facade is complex and was started in his childhood when he rejected the guidance or dominion of his parents or extended family. He began to develop and play roles to reduce punishment and gain acceptance. In effect, he has replaced his feelings with roles he thinks the world will find acceptable. For his survival, he cannot allow anyone, not even himself, to discover his real, vulnerable self.

His facade protects him from consequences by providing a respectable front. The batterer typically appears calm, reasonable, successful, and non-violent. Because all batterers are not the same, without extensive analysis it is impossible to tell how much a particular batterer's interaction with the world is a facade. Initially, it is impossible to tell how dangerous he might be since many of his maladaptions to his failures and deficits take place in secret.

The abusive man may appear truthful and maybe even healthy, but he is not. In public only his best side shows. He is always ready to do battle, to

Change is the Third Path
M. Lindsey, R. McBride and C. Platt

show strength and to control. People often see him as interesting and wish to be with him, because his front is very engaging, yet he dare not let people know him. In reality he is a very fragile person. He does not feel safe being close. He fears he really has nothing to offer people and that they will be disappointed and leave him. This man is driven by emotional needs and pain he neither understands nor takes the time to examine. He does not think about why he does what he does or about the consequences of his actions.

His facade hides fear, shame, guilt, rage, and even perversion. He fears discovery, that the world will find out that he has been "faking it." His low self-esteem will not permit him to believe he may be bright or talented or to disclose that he feels afraid and powerless.

The front hides the real self that harbors his goals and wishes, of which society is unaware. These wishes might include the desire to rape and murder women, to frequent lower class bars with prostitutes, to have sex with other men, to be a hero, saving the world or his family, or to be able to seduce any woman.

These fantasies help the abusive man avoid his inauthenticity. Reflected in the fantasies is the real person, a man who is and has been alienated from society and his family, an angry man who feels that no matter how hard he tries, he will never succeed.

Like all men, what the abusive man wants is to have some success at the goals he has set for himself. These goals include loving and caring for a mate and family, being a capable and successful worker, living up to masculine values about protecting family and country, and enjoying a happy life.

What he actually achieves in his life is something quite different. As an adult he resists any feedback that does not match his internal perceptions, goals, or agenda. Eventually he will suffer the consequences of failing to respond to the rules of human interaction. As he goes through life, his problems mount, defeats accrue, and losses increase. His employer, friends, family, and social institutions become increasingly punishing as they grow weary of trying to help him. He fails to get promotions, friends leave him, his mate flees because he remains unavailable emotionally and often physically. He will miss experiencing some of the rewards of human interaction which make life more fulfilling. He does not learn from the consequences but rather finds reasons to blame others for his behavior.

He starts over with new promises and hopes, only to repeat the process. As a young man, he is able to start over, to hide his failures and losses. As he gets older, his ability to hide from the truth diminishes and his ability to recover emotionally from the loss of self-worth becomes increasingly limited. In the end he may commit suicide or homicide, die early from alcohol, drugs, stress, or disease, or lead a meaningless existence.

Sadly the abusive man often has a lot to offer but it is buried so deep that even he does not see or believe his potential. In some cases he feels and cares more than many of the people around him, yet he will not expose this soft side to the world because of his fear of being vulnerable. The loving and caring part him is hidden by his unpredictability, violence, and unresponsiveness to others. People around him come to regard the abusive man as cold, aloof, distant, self-centered, hard, unavailable, and rigid.

Repressed feelings

Inherent in the masculine role is the belief that a man's feelings are better left unexpressed. Underlying this belief is the idea that expressing feelings is a sign of weakness, hence leaves one vulnerable to attack. Yet it is the failure to express one's emotions that leads to violence. The repression of feelings is a critical problem for all men, but especially for the batterer, who is less in touch with his feelings than most men. When he was a child, he shut off his internal world because it was too painful and confusing. He relies on traditional male roles because they allow him to avoid the pain of consciousness.

The abusive man has learned to block his emotional pain by ignoring it or pushing it aside and moving into anger, rage or violence. Experience from working with this kind of man shows that he can express thoughts but he cannot express feelings. His practiced substitutes of anger and rage are ingrained to the point that his feelings are unrecognizable to him as are the feelings of others. He has little empathy. He cannot take care of himself or nurture others emotionally. He talks about sex as though it were a mechanical act. As long as he disallows feelings of sadness, hurt, fear, guilt, embarrassment, weakness, loss and other "unacceptable" male feelings, the abusive man will continue to have a high potential for violence.

Closely tied to men's repression of feelings is their jealousy. Many abusive men say that they feel jealous when they feel hurt, demeaned, or afraid. Men in general want to see women as sexually available, but this fantasy is threatening to abusive men with mates. If other women are available, maybe their wives are also. The abusive man who is jealous has a tremendous difficulty not fantasizing about his mate engaging in sex with other men. This jealousy is based on fear that he cannot keep his mate or from projection of his own desires for an affair or the reality of his ongoing affairs..

The dilemma for the abusive man is between risking rejection if his feelings are expressed or experiencing frustration and violence if his feelings go unexpressed. The irony is that without the ability to feel and express sadness and hurt one is not as able to feel and express happiness and joy.

Hatred of women

The notion exists for many men that women are somehow less than men. This belief is even held by a large number of women. For example, until

Change is the Third Path
M. Lindsey, R. McBride and C. Platt

recently it was a popular male belief that women were unable and should not be allowed to do a "man's job." There was and is much resentment over women entering the last professional male bastions: fire fighting, the military, criminal justice, law and management.

It is doubtful that a good relationship can exist when one person looks down on another. As one man put it, "Women are just walking, talking life support systems for a pussy." As long as men see women as objects to use for gratification of needs rather than as equals, violence will persist.

The man who batters has hatred. He takes out his hatred on the woman he loves. This occurs for several reasons: he has been trained to hate women; he experiences his dependency as arising from his mate's control; he has so much self-hatred that it must be directed outward or be turned in on himself; and he has hatred for those who have hurt him. Regardless of the actual source, the hatred is often directed outward at those most vulnerable, typically at his mate or children, because he can attack them with fewer consequences. The abusive man also attacks the people closest to him because those people have the capacity to injure him. Loved ones have gotten past his defenses. He is vulnerable to them.

Although much of his destructive behavior comes from distrust and hatred, the batterer often denies that he feels hatred. The abusive man can talk about distrusting women or putting women on pedestals but seldom can he admit to hate. Sometimes, the general distrust and hatred of all women will get focused on one woman. If the man perceives he loves this woman and feels she has betrayed him, the woman is at grave risk of serious injury or death.

The man who feels trapped by his emotional dependency on women and believes his mate controls him is at risk of becoming abusive when the relationship becomes permanent. He is trapped and controlled not by her behavior but by his own dependency needs and beliefs about how men are supposed to be. He attributes power to his mate but eventually comes to hate her because he believes she took control. He wants closeness and permanence but does not know how to deal with it. The violent man often perceives his mate as withholding something valuable—love, sex or recognition.

No doubt much of the hatred the abusive man feels is toward himself. He is trapped by his beliefs about how men are supposed to be. He feels inadequate as a provider, protector, husband, father, or man. He often loathes himself because of his passivity. He wants closeness and permanence but does not know how to deal with it. He lacks the capacity to communicate his needs or set limits, yet he is unable to admit any of this. He turns his self-hate outward by belittling or striking out at his mate.

Undependable or over responsible

In our society one of the features of men's roles is responsibility for their family's physical and financial welfare. They also are assigned roles as leaders and teachers. Many feel responsible for teaching their families the best way of doing things. Logically, if a person accepts responsibility for something, control must accompany the acceptance. This is the premise all men, not just abusive men, operate from. "I am responsible, therefore, I must have control." From this an interesting paradox develops. While many women report being controlled by men, many men feel they are without control most of the time. They feel responsible for people and events over which they have no real control because men are supposed to have the wisdom or skill to solve most all problems.

And their feelings are well-founded. Social inequities in education and health care along with uncertainty in the job market threaten the security of many American families. The cult of individualism and overemphasis on competition rather than cooperation impose real burdens on all but the best nurtured and most skilled. For the man who comes from the best of homes, performing the traditional masculine role is a difficult task. For the man who was abused physically and emotionally, the task is overwhelming. The abusive man often makes an effort to be responsible for everything concerning his family. He assumes responsibility for too much. Sharing decision-making is not a concept he understands, so his mate is left out of the process. He is trapped between his dependency needs and his sense of duty. He may give to an extreme—either too much or not enough. He promises to give everything, then feels resentful and frightened because in actuality he can give very little. The more he feels himself failing in traditional roles, the more likely he is to attack his mate, run away, or push her away through his violence.

Abusive men do not have a well-developed sense of personal responsibility, either. If asked "Who is responsible for my behavior?" most adults would respond that they are responsible for themselves. Most people would consider themselves capable of making moral or rational decisions and therefore, answerable for their behavior. The abusive man might respond similarly but his actions are different. His unspoken belief is that his behavior is controlled by something outside himself.

The man who abuses believes and acts as though some external force or person can make him secure, happy, prosperous, and loved. As a child, he tried to gain these things from his parents but repeatedly failed. As an adult, he believes these are bestowed by his mate, children, friends, society or God/fate.

The abusive man feels a deep need to be taken care of and is unable to admit this to himself. Consequently, he feels betrayed when he finds himself in a relationship where his mate asks for affection and support but

Change is the Third Path
M. Lindsey, R. McBride and C. Platt

is unable to take away his pain. He wants his mate to do something to make him happy and feel secure just like the movie and television romances promise. When this doesn't happen, this man believes the failure is her fault because she did not "do it right." He believed the Big Lie, that being in a permanent relationship will solve the problems of pain, isolation, or feelings of worthlessness. (Women also report falling victim to this belief.) What he does not understand or accept is that he is the only one who can resolve those feelings. That is, he is the only one responsible for his happiness.

By blaming others for his problems, he can avoid looking to himself for answers. As long as he blames others, he can deny responsibility for his life and maintain that his belief system is correct. He also has an excuse to abuse others because he has identified them as at fault for his hurt.

Irrational beliefs

The abusive man hits when he perceives he has been injured. His violence is the result of perceived injury. When he feels hurt, he strikes back. He is hurt easily. He is fragile even though he may not show this side to the world.

The abusive man's way of thinking is based on irrational or unreasonable ideas, expectations or rules. It is easy for him to fail in relationships. He has catastrophic thoughts when his mate doesn't behave the way he thought she should have.

> "If my mate disagrees with me, it means she does not love me."
> "If my mate disagrees with me, it means she does not respect me."
> "My mate cannot change."
> "No matter what I do, it will not be good enough."

Obviously, irrational thoughts make it very difficult to have a fair and rational argument.

If these thoughts reflect reality, his best option is to leave. However, an abusive man often constructs this idea from misperceptions.

Other irrational beliefs that the abusive man holds are that if he does anything wrong he won't be caught and if he gets caught, he'll be able to avoid consequences. Many abusive men believe that no one has the right to impose limits on them. Authority is a force to be resisted.

Abusive men employ minimization, denial and distortion of reality. The following dialogue illustrates how the abusive man minimizes the level of abuse or denies that it happened.

> "He chased me up and down Colfax Avenue at speeds of fifty miles an hour. We made U-turns and went through red lights," the woman said angrily.

"I did not chase her," the man responded.

"You did, too," the woman maintained.

"No, I did not," the man argued.

"Did you go up and down Colfax Avenue at high speeds? Did you make U-turns and run red lights?" the therapist then asked the man.

"Yes, we did," the man answered.

"Then what was it you did if it was not chasing?" asked the therapist.

"I was following her and just wanted to talk," the man responded.

Since this man had been extremely violent, there was no reason this woman should have wanted to stop and chat. By changing the word "chase" to "follow" the man eliminated, in his mind, the threatening aspect of his behavior. After all, he "just wanted to talk." Abusive men blame the victim, distort the truth, and lie outright about what transpired.

Over-stimulation and chaos

To the outside world, the abusive man usually appears calm and organized, he has good moments when he feels successful, loved, and connected yet his feelings of not really belonging persist. His internal world is a jumble of activities and feelings, thus it is always easier for him to be on his way somewhere else—another job, town, woman or project—than it is to maintain what is already accomplished. If he lets the level of stimulation drop, he feels his confusion and emptiness. Desperately driven to avoid his internal world and ignore the wreckage that he has left behind, he goes through life cut off from both his internal and external worlds. Accurate feedback could salvage his life but he finds learning the truth too painful so he develops methods to avoid hearing it.

To survive this emptiness he requires something to focus on. Often obsession fills the void. He decides what is needed in order to "feel good" and then pursues this with great energy. The stimulation can be sex, work, sports, drugs, alcohol, or a fantasy world. The stimulation often replaces any real human contact and may temporarily patch the hole he feels inside. The chaos he builds also helps displace the sense of failure he may feel over being unsuccessful at work, unable to protect mate and family, or desperately unhappy.

If his obsession turns out to be a woman, things will go well for a while. However, his internal demand for pain reduction and lack of relationship skills will eventually exceed the ability of the relationship to alleviate the pain. In his desire to avoid his pain, he may drink, gamble, drive away family and friends, lose his job, get into "hassles" everywhere, destroy property, and/or hit his children. Unable or unwilling to acknowledge his

Change is the Third Path
M. Lindsey, R. McBride and C. Platt

responsibility for bad choices and unreal expectations, he will blame others, chiefly his mate. When the pain becomes unbearable, he will attack.

The abusive man has goals and agendas unknown to others and marches toward them with little regard for other people's ideas, wants, or needs. But he cannot admit this because he cannot see it. The lens through which he could have observed himself was distorted by the experiences of his childhood. He grew up being two people: the facade he shows the world and the real self he feels inside. He keeps himself stimulated to avoid his internal conflict and pain.

Alienation

The abusive man perceives the world as hostile and dangerous. It is a place that at any moment could bring him physical harm, embarrassment, ridicule or rejection. He feels at risk all the time and is continually on guard to protect himself from attack.

He tries to build relationships and has some success, but because he distrusts people, he tries to keep them at a safe distance. He separates himself from other people with overwork, alcohol, drugs or sex. He is unskilled in making and keeping the friendships and human connections that would help him develop a well-balanced life. He is prone to long, involved, obsessive arguments that never lead to resolutions. He fights with the people around him. The fights may not be physical, but they are hostile and defensive interactions that leave him feeling betrayed and angry. People tire of his behavior and become indifferent or unfriendly. Eventually, he destroys many relationships through overt aggression or passive resistance and finds himself increasingly isolated.

When someone points out his irrational behavior he rejects the feedback, identifying the critic rather than his own behavior as the source of his difficulties.

Since the abusive man may not be able to ask for what he wants directly, he bears the pain of his unmet needs. He misunderstands his feelings of hurt and sadness and says to himself, "I am strong enough to take it." He continues stuffing hurt until ultimately he feels so used, betrayed, and unjustly attacked that he explodes in self righteous anger that too often escalates into violence.

Fear of abandonment

Despite his attempts, however well intentioned, to portray the self-confident male, the abusive man knows the person he *is* must be hidden. When finally he finds a person to love and with whom he can have a relationship, it initially provides an immense relief from his life-long isolation. His relief is short-lived, for an intense fear of loss begins to dominate his life. He lives in fear that someone will take his beloved away or that she will leave as soon as his real self is revealed.

Some men believe they can hold their mates by being giving, endlessly attentive or by providing unlimited money. Nevertheless, their fear at losing control persists. The woman may meet another man, lose interest, resist being the focus of such intense attention or develop additional interests outside the relationship (which, in part, may account for the increase in abuse during pregnancy). The suspicion that she is involved with another man may cause him to follow her to the store or spy on her at work. In extreme cases he may imprison her in the house. Although he may not fear a rival, he may think she requires more than he can provide: more feelings, more stability, more companionship. Perhaps he is afraid she will leave because he pressures her to change, to be something more than she can be: thinner, smarter, better looking.

By focusing on the relationship as the solution to his unhappiness, the abusive man has attributed to his mate the power to fill his emptiness. Of course, she cannot do this. The more he struggles to get her to be what he needs to relieve his pain and inadequacy, the less satisfaction he derives. She may try desperately to satisfy his needs, but she cannot be the source of his healing.

Obsessiveness

Many people have described the abusive man as impulsive. He is actually incredibly obsessive. He fixates on a goal, agenda, plan, or thought and becomes overwhelmed by it. He is commonly a narrow individual and can become obsessed with anything: making money, a job, an activity or a relationship. There are times when all of us become engrossed in a project or subject, but the abusive man is driven.

Feelings and thoughts go around and around inside his head, gradually taking control of his entire life and eliminating other activities such as quiet times with his mate/family, creative endeavors or volunteer work. He angrily resists interference with his pursuits.

When he focuses on getting or keeping a woman, his obsessive behavior can lead to violence or homicide. While not every batterer has an obsession with needing to have one particular woman, it is a common theme. Sometimes the abusive man becomes obsessive about getting even with his mate for some perceived humiliation or betrayal. Whether his obsession involves getting her back or getting even, he may find himself unable to work, eat or sleep. He spends much of his time thinking about the situation and how he can get what he wants.

Inability to handle criticism

Under the hardness of the violent man lies extreme sensitivity to perceived slights. In fact, the abusive man is so fragile he finds criticism almost intolerable. The most devastating result of the physical or emotional abuse of male children is their rejection of external authority and feedback. Male children who were abused and grow up to batter have made a decision to maintain as much control over their lives as possible. Because they view

Change is the Third Path
M. Lindsey, R. McBride and C. Platt

others as basically hostile and dangerous, they do all they can to avoid any individual's or institution's influence in their lives.

While this rejection of control by abusive people is a wise choice for the abused child, it means he will be alone and at war with his world if he is not able to find other nurturing adults he can trust. A child who grows into an alienated adult cannot tolerate information that contradicts his view of the world. He perceives information as criticism and criticism feels like an attack. He does not understand that there can be more than one solution to a question or a problem. He operates on the idea that almost everything is black or white, good or bad, right or wrong, with very little gray area. If a solution different than his is suggested, he might feel wrong, bad, stupid, humiliated and not in control. He feels a great need to defend himself and shift responsibility. Because he is unable to take feedback, he cannot correct his behaviors through normal interaction with other people. He remains stuck in destructive patterns of behavior.

Violence as a lifestyle

The likelihood that someone will be violent depends upon the interaction between four factors: culture, personal history, individual choice and biology. Permission to use violence is given to men through gender training and parental modeling. See Violence Model on the next page.

Biologically some men may be predisposed to violence because of brain damage or chromosomal abnormalities. The broader culture permits men to use violence in certain situations: protection of country, family and self. Local custom may sanction other uses of violence: to enforce racial or sexual bias, for example. Families model uses of violence, and if a man is reared in a family where violence against and between family members is condoned and he sees few other models of behavior, he may repeat the lessons he was taught. Regardless of environment, individuals do have choices and upon reflection about the kinds of lives and families they as adults want to have, may choose to treat others with respect. Respect, however, like violence, is learned and the more deprivation and abuse people suffer, the more likely they are to be abusive.

There are many men who grow up in families and in neighborhoods where predatory violence is a way of life. If they are injured and do not avenge the injury, they are marked as prey. When this pattern extends to his own family, a man is at higher risk for becoming abusive. Growing up, he was forced to accept the abuse given him. Most often, it came from people whom he wanted to trust and love. Being abused created in him a strong need to protect himself and to control all aspects of his world. When he grows up and finds a mate, he carries with him the responses he has developed to deal with hurt: withdrawal and attack.

The literature on abusive men indicates that all men who batter were not abused nor did they all witness violence in the home. However long term therapy helps the men recognize or remember abuse.

For instance, after years of therapy one man remembered his father "grabbing my step-mother by the hair and slamming her face into the table, breaking her nose." Prior to this he reported a "wonderful childhood." Men underreport incidents of sibling abuse, incest, rape, criticism and neglect.

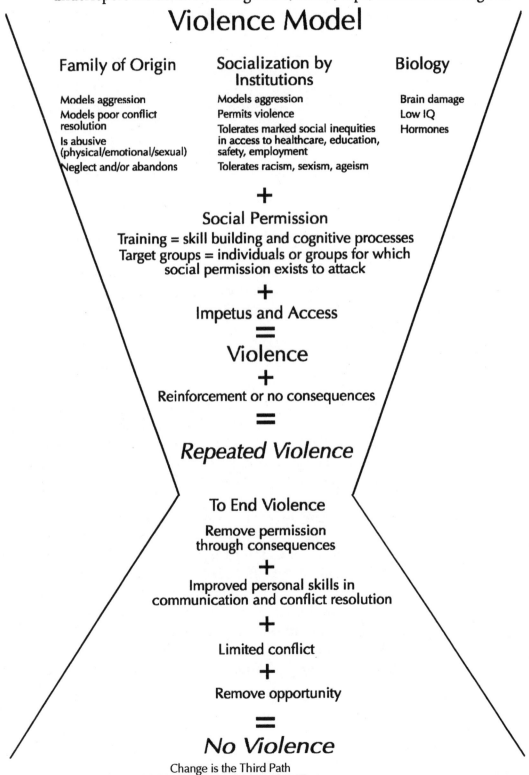

Violence Model

Family of Origin	Socialization by Institutions	Biology
Models aggression	Models aggression	Brain damage
Models poor conflict resolution	Permits violence	Low IQ
Is abusive (physical/emotional/sexual)	Tolerates marked social inequities in access to healthcare, education, safety, employment	Hormones
Neglect and/or abandons	Tolerates racism, sexism, ageism	

+

Social Permission

Training = skill building and cognitive processes
Target groups = individuals or groups for which social permission exists to attack

+

Impetus and Access

=

Violence

+

Reinforcement or no consequences

=

Repeated Violence

To End Violence

Remove permission through consequences

+

Improved personal skills in communication and conflict resolution

+

Limited conflict

+

Remove opportunity

=

No Violence

Change is the Third Path
M. Lindsey, R. McBride and C. Platt

Therapy and Stabilization

Beliefs are... either effective or ineffective tools for living. The pertinent question is, do your beliefs maximize self-respect and pleasure in living? Little else matters. Woolfolk and Richardson, *Stress, Sanity & Survival.* 1978

Men who are violent must deal with a variety of issues to use therapy effectively. Therapy requires change. How much change is necessary or desired is an individual matter requiring personal choices.

For people who batter, therapy can be divided into three phases. The first is stabilization, the second is extended management and third is recovery. To begin the process of stabilization, you must understand and make a commitment to several important values if you want to make changes that will be significant and lasting.

Accountability

As a domestic violence perpetrator you must be willing to accept total responsibility for your choice to use abuse and violence to solve problems. The victim may or may not be a source of the conflict in which you are involved but she is *not* responsible for the abuse and violence you directed at her. You need to stop blaming your partner and minimizing and denying the abuse and violence you have committed toward her.

Admitting that your life is not okay and that your view of it may be distorted are probably the last things you want to do. If you are able to acknowledge the problems in your life, it is likely you will claim they were created by others and that, given a little more time, you will be able to work them out. If you use abusive and violent behavior to resolve problems, you probably put the responsibility for your behavior on your victim. Although you made the choice to use violence to resolve conflict, it is likely that you neither want nor believe you deserve consequences for your behavior. But as long as you can avoid consequences, you will continue to be abusive and violent.

The core of real change is accountability.

As you read the *Basics of Accountability below (adapted from Barbara Hart's Accountability Standards)* ask yourself the following questions:

> How do I feel when I read each line of the basics?
> Do I try to cover up the truth?
> Can I tell another person about my behavior and if not, why?
> Am I going to begin telling the truth about my behavior?
> Is it right or possible to acknowledge each statement and if not, why?
> Will I be accountable for my behavior and if not, why?
> Do I intend to be abusive or violent again?

If you answered *no* to the second to last question above (Will I be accountable for my behavior ...) then, therapy will be difficult, if not a waste of time and money.

If you answered *yes* to the last question (Do I intend to be abusive and violent again?) you have no hope yet of gaining control of your life.

If you assume responsibility for your behavior regardless of real or imagined justifications for it, you can begin the process of recovery. Committing yourself to living abuse- and violence-free will require expenditures of time, energy and money.

After you have read the *Basics of Accountability* evaluate again your answers on the *Behavioral* and *Stalking Behavior Checklists*.

Basics of Accountability

✔ I have been abusive and violent and may be again in the future.

✔ I used abuse and violence to control or punish my partner and others.

✔ Abusive and violent behavior was my choice for resolving conflict.

✔ My behavior was out of control and it was inexcusable and sometimes criminal.

✔ I cannot blame my abusive and violent behavior on others' provoking me.

✔ I am solely responsible for choosing abusive and violent behavior to resolve conflict.

✔ I cannot blame my abusive and violent behavior on stress, jealousy, chemical dependency, childhood training or on my childhood abuse.

✔ I must identify all the abusive and violent acts which I perpetrated.

✔ I must identify the pain and losses inflicted on my partner and others.

- ✔ I am sorry for and regret my abusive and violent behavior and the suffering I inflicted on my partner and others.

- ✔ I must attempt to make amends to those I hurt without infringing on their lives.

- ✔ I acknowledge that my partner and others may be afraid of me and may not trust me, possibly forever.

- ✔ I do not expect or deserve forgiveness from my partner or others.

- ✔ There was nothing in my relationships that caused me to be abusive and violent. Therefore, I must work on myself for the rest of my life to prevent a reoccurrence of my destructive behavior.

Denial

Part of the process of becoming accountable and stable is to stop denying your problems and to start admitting that you need help. Almost every person who enters therapy starts in the same place—a state of denial. Indeed, for most abusive and violent people, the thought of attending a group session can be terrifying and stressful. It is easy to rationalize away the need for therapy. There are ample excuses people have used to avoid seeking help.

It's a private problem

"This is a private problem between her and me and it's none of their fucking business" is a common reply the abusive man gives when confronted about his violence. Really? Ask yourself these questions.

How are the children affected by the fighting?
Are the relatives involved or looking the other way?
Are the neighbors deaf and blind?
Am I sure no one hears the yelling and screaming or sees the bruises?
Have the police been involved yet?
How private is my life in divorce court?
How private is being arrested for battery?
How private is my problem if I make the news for killing her?

The cost of domestic violence to society in medical expense, lost productivity, and emotionally crippled children is staggering. It is not a private problem, it is a global problem. You just haven't done anything positive about it yet.

I'm different

Often the abusive man professes he is completely different and doesn't belong with "these" kinds of men.

Does all my effort to make my life work seem worth it and do I feel happy with my life?
Do I feel frustrated or threatened by the world and my mate?
Do I feel powerless to control all the things for which I am responsible?
Do I feel the world is unfair toward me?
Do I feel like I keep moving faster just to stay even?

You are a unique individual, but you have a lot in common with other violent men. Every member of an abuse and violence group feels frustrated, powerless, justified in his violence, mistreated, harried and victimized.

My situation is different

"I am not like those guys. I am not really abusive."
"I just screamed and threw something."
"I just pushed her; I didn't hit her."
"I only hit her once and it won't happen again."
"She was hysterical and I was just trying to snap her back into control."
"It was an accident; I only lost control for a few minutes."
"I just need to learn to handle this situation."
"I didn't really mean it and besides she forgave me."

Abuse and violence are purposeful behaviors aimed at gaining control. If you acted out violently, you made a deliberate choice aimed at a specific goal. You made that choice because it works for you.

I'm okay

"I like myself the way I am. There is nothing wrong with me" is another claim of some abusive men. If there is nothing wrong, why are you abusing your mate?

The abusive and violent man often believes no one can help him. Even if there is help, he does not want someone trying to "brainwash" him.

You need to understand that a therapist cannot fix or change you. A therapist can help you with change but the choices and changes are up to you to make. You have to decide if you want to change your behavior and when and how to do it.

I'm hopeless

"I'm a hopeless fuck up."
"I can't change, so why try?"
"I'm incompetent."
"I'm stupid."
"I probably deserve to be unhappy and miserable."

Maybe you were taught as a child that you were incompetent and stupid. You probably tried desperately to please your parents, but failed so often you learned to doubt your capabilities. You may have decided early in life to reject whatever you heard from your crazy world, and you developed rules of your own. These haven't been very effective guidelines. If you work at therapy, you can develop a new set of guides for yourself, you can change and be happier. But you cannot do it by yourself.

It's her problem

Numerous abusive and violent men allege, "My mate has a problem. If she would change, everything would be okay." You may believe this but if it is so, ask yourself these questions:

Why am I still with her?
Why do I choose to stay in an unhappy situation?
How many problems have I had in my other intimate relationships?
Am I so dependent I must try to control her and make her be what I want with violence?

Your mate may have behaviors you do not like and that may hurt you, but you also have a problem—using violent and abusive behaviors.

I don't have money or *I don't have time*

"I can't afford therapy and I don't have the time" is an almost universal declaration of abusive and violent men.

How much money and time have I spent separating repeatedly?
How much will it cost before I am finished with a divorce?
How much will it cost me for drinks or drugs to deaden my pain?
How much will it cost me in pain and suffering?
How much have I budgeted for a new gun and other "toys" but not for therapy?
How much time can I spend feeling hurt, betrayed, abandoned, angry and in continuous chaos?

She is gone

"She left and will not return, so why bother?" What about my next relationship? You will repeat what just ended if your cycle of abuse and violence is not broken.

She is back

"We can work it out, so why bother?"
How many times have we tried to work it out?
How many times have I made promises to change?
Why do I keep feeling she will leave again?
Why am I doing this for her?
Why not start therapy for myself?

It's too painful

"It is too painful and I don't want to deal with it."
Real men don't cry.
Once I give in to the pain, I'll be wiped out.
I don't feel a thing.

Therapy requires taking risks and is sometimes emotionally painful but no more painful than the struggle you are involved in. There are no instant answers but if you stay with the process you can find some concrete solutions.

Accepting Information and Forming Therapeutic Relationships

As an abusive and violent person you have limited capacity to accept feedback or information from others. You are so fragile, so sensitive that you cannot tolerate contradiction of your view of the world. You can't tolerate much—if any—criticism and reject it. Already fragile, you interpret any comments about your ideas or behavior as an attack.

You probably do not understand that there can be more than one approach to a question or a problem. You assume that almost everything is black or white, good or bad, right or wrong—there is very little gray area. If someone differs with you, you may feel wrong, bad, stupid, humiliated or not in control. Your inability to listen to criticism creates conflict and a major problem for you.

As an abusive man you shut off feedback because you cannot trust its source, especially if the source is someone close. However, making changes requires that you incorporate new ideas into your life. If therapy is to be successful, you must learn to become open to feedback. Without outside feedback you are locked into an isolated world with no help available. When you begin to allow others to teach you, you can begin to experience success.

Developing and maintaining a trusting relationship with the therapist and other men involved in the process of recovery is critical at all stages of therapy. In order to stabilize and make lasting change, you need strategies. The therapist must be able to suggest new methods of dealing with your life.

You need to be open to new feelings, ideas, values, and methods for managing conflict. This will require that you be open to ideas from other people, especially your therapist. The therapist may say things to you or ask you questions that cause hurt or pressure. You may feel that the therapist is asking you to try something that is frightening or unreasonable. This does not mean the therapist wishes to make you over into a version of him or herself or to dominate and control you. The therapist is engaging you in a process that is difficult. This process challenges the ideas, values, attitudes and behaviors that are destructive to your life. If you reject this challenge, the therapeutic process will fail.

Finish the following sentences about your therapeutic process.

I don't belong in therapy because _____

I don't trust the therapist because_____

I don't trust the group because _____

Therapy won't work for me because_____

I feel uncomfortable in therapy because _____

I don't want to make any changes in the following areas: _____

I am afraid of therapy because _____

I want to accomplish the following in therapy _____

_____

Group Process and Other Basic Tools

**Group
process**

The opening stages of therapy are designed to teach you to contain your violence, teach you basic skills, and introduce the process of emotional healing and recovery. You need to understand three things to make the group process work for you:

> Violence is wrong and criminal.
> Your life is unmanageable.
> The group and therapist are sources of help.

You may resent being confronted about your abuse, violence and other forms of chaos in your life. The purpose of confrontation is to help you become accountable. Only by being accountable can you end your abuse and violence and have stability in your life.

To make the group work for you and the other members:

Show up for the group regularly. If you do not attend regularly, you have denied yourself input to and feedback from the group. You also risk being removed from the group.

Show up on time. Being late is obviously disruptive to the group process.

Be as honest and open as you can. This includes questioning group members' beliefs and actions that seem inappropriate or destructive.

Use words that clearly express how you feel. Statements like "pissed off" or "not worth a shit" are vague. If you use words like *angry, hostile, frustrated, sad, afraid, lonely* or *happy*, which are more specific, people will better understand how you feel.

Practice making "I" statements rather than "you" statements. You are taking responsibility for your life when you make "I" statements such as, "I feel sad" or "I feel hurt" or "I am angry." You are probably not taking responsibility for your life but are blaming others for your problems when you make "you" statements such as, "You make me angry" or "You screwed everything up." If the concept seems strange, work with your therapist and the group on it.

Respect other group members' feelings and ideas and expect group members to respect your feelings and ideas. The group is a good place to express anger and other feelings. However, it is not a place to act out on others.

How to use the group

Although each therapist will structure the group in a way he or she feels is most beneficial to you, the following example may help your understanding of the process.

Early group sessions might be tightly structured and start with a check-in by each man. *Each man responds for three minutes:*

If you are experiencing a crisis, say so.
Tell how you are feeling.
Give a brief summary of significant events in your week. (Any violence or near violent outbursts. If not, why not?)
Indicate if you do (or don't) need group time after check-in to discuss your feelings and problems.

After check-in, those who need it take time to share their issues, problems, or feelings with the group.

If you are afraid or ashamed and do not ask for help, you will not get it.
If you sit back and hide, your life will remain unmanageable.
If you wait until there is "time" because you think other group members need more help, you will not get help.

The speaker listens to the feedback from the group—fears, expectations, hopes, and goals.

Feedback is not just advice or criticism. It is information that the therapist or group provides to help you.

Feedback exercise: You might need to learn how to give and receive feedback. Watch how the facilitator is giving direct feedback to members. Ask to practice by going around the group circle naming each group member and stating one significant thing you have learned about that person.

Group discussion

Listen, ask questions. Contribute your information and ideas. Help move the discussion along. Point out if others monopolize the discussion. Confront the therapist if he or she says something you don't understand or with which you disagree.

Change is the Third Path
M. Lindsey, R. McBride and C. Platt

Close the group with some ritual such as having each man express:

What I got out of group today.
What I wanted, didn't get and why I didn't get it.
How I get my needs met. What stops me?
How my denial works and how I can overcome it.

Think of the group members as mirrors that reflect to you things you don't see or deny about yourself.

List Five Personal Topics
I Would Like to Talk About in Group

For example: I would like to understand why I get so angry about some things.

1. _____
_____

2. _____
_____

3. _____
_____

4. _____
_____

5. _____
_____

The Cycle of Violence

A goal of treatment is to help you analyze, understand, learn to manage and finally resolve your anger. You can quickly begin to understand how rage develops, but resolving it is far more difficult. You must learn specific techniques to manage your anger when it arises during the course of therapy. Identifying the process through which conflict escalates into violence is the first step in managing your anger.

You may want to resist the fact that healing demands that you take responsibility for your abuse and violence. You may want to make statements such as, "She made me do it." "She asked for it." "I was drunk." "I didn't know what I was doing." "It was an accident." "I won't ever do it again."

But before you resist too long, remind yourself that abuse and violence are tools that many men use—tools that help men control women and protect themselves from emotional pain. Abuse and violence appear to work, at least in the short term. But what they appear to accomplish—changing a situation or someone's behavior—does not effectively decrease your emotional pain. Without intervention and treatment, you will probably continue to repeat your abuse and violence and become increasingly violent.

It is clear that a boy raised in an abusive and violent family is more likely to be violent as an adult than a boy raised in a home where conflict is resolved reasonably. Girls from violent homes are at greater risk of being victims. Without intervention and treatment, the abusive and violent behaviors you model for your children may continue as your children become the next generation of victims and perpetrators. Is that the legacy you want to leave your children?

A good way to begin to change is by understanding your cycle of violence. As you read about each stage, recall your own feelings as your anger builds.

Tension-building phase

The cycle is probably a continuous process for you. Although you probably have feelings of satisfaction that occasionally relieve your pressure, in the long run, your dissatisfaction with life adds more pressure than is relieved. You may not recognize or understand how you build tension until you finally explode in rage. To start, you need to identify the conflicts and unresolved issues that create stress for you. Then begin identifying the body signs and thoughts you associate with the tension.

Learn what external and internal stressors affect you.

> External stressors can include traffic, noise, family needs, demands at work, money problems, criticism, relating job to personal success, being late, making mistakes, being told what to do.

> Internal stressors may include lack of confidence, jealous interpretations, feelings of failure, need to control in situations beyond your control, being over or under responsible, or feelings of inadequacy.

Situations become stressors when you try to avoid conflict, lack assertiveness, lack personal boundaries, use inappropriate personal skills or behaviors, blame, fail to recognize your responsibility for the stress. It is important for you to understand that your tension is caused by your inability to deal with the external stress and that your tension builds because of your own internal stressors—what you believe about yourself.

Tony described his tension by using the beat of a snare drum as a metaphor:

> My life has always felt like it was full of pressure. Normally, the drum inside my brain was a slow tap . . . tap. As the pressure continued to build, the drum would begin to beat faster until it was a full-blown drum roll. Then I knew I was in trouble, out of control, racing down a path of destruction I didn't want to be on. I didn't know how to stop

the drum from beating. The faster it got, the more frightened I became until I exploded into a rage.

The following story with minor variations has been told so many times by different men that it is a classic example of how men can escalate their tension to an explosion.

Saturday Martin only worked half instead of a full day. He got home about 11:15 in the morning. He knew his wife got off work at noon on Saturdays, so he thought that they could go for a drive in the mountains and find a nice place to have a late lunch.

About twelve-thirty, he had a beer and began to fret that she was hanging around talking with the women after work. He saw that the trip to the mountains would be wrecked if she didn't get home soon. He began thinking repeatedly, "God damn it, if she doesn't quit screwing around and get home she is going to fuck up the whole day."

About one o'clock he began to worry that she had got into an automobile accident. He was pacing the floor and continuously looking out the door to see if he could see the car coming down the street. Then he began to think, "She probably wrecked the fucking car. God damn her. Maybe she got hurt. Maybe she is dead. Ah, shit where is she?"

By one-thirty he was frantic, had smashed his empty beer bottle against the wall and started drinking another beer. Now his thoughts were, "God damn, fucking bitch is probably out screwing someone. I knew it. I knew I couldn't trust the fucking whore. God damn bitch, she better not fuck with me."

Close to two o'clock his wife arrived and was surprised to find him home. His response was, "Where the fuck have you been, God damn it?"

"I just went to the damn mall to look at a few things because I didn't think you would be home until later."

"Bullshit, you were probably out fucking somebody, weren't you? Tell me the fucking truth, God damn you," as he pushed her with both hands and slammed her against the wall. He continued until his rage was spent.

Your tension escalates because you are not getting your needs met—companionship, recreation, affection, rest. You fear being hurt and abandoned and you need to gain control.

In your thoughts, you probably repeat negative self talk—"No matter how much I try, I'm no good." "I never get anything." "Nobody cares"— as well as ruminating over what you see as life's failures. If you do not deal with your emotional pain and repressed feelings, your feelings of fear, hurt, anxiety, tension and anger will increase until you are in a blind rage.

Explosion phase

An explosion can occur anywhere from minutes to several months after you feel conflict.

Because you do not recognize your stressors and have no plan to confront and resolve your feelings of anxiety, fear, hurt and pain, your tension increases until it reaches a critical point and you explode. The "reason" or excuse you use for striking out does not matter. You may use alcohol as a catalyst to reach the explosive point or you may become enraged because your mate "looks at you wrong." You have mentally turned her into an object that is causing you pain. Because you want the pain to stop, you strike out at her in an effort to make her change or to punish her for causing you pain.

Acknowledge the fact that you explode and the many different ways to you explode—verbally, emotionally and physically.

Can you identify the danger and lethality of this phase?
Can you identify the feelings that accompany your explosion?

Think about your explosion.

Does it eliminate your tension or does it only relieve some of the pressure?
Does it solve your problems or create more?

Since you are probably building tension most of the time, it is dangerous for you to assume that because an explosion has occurred things will be calm for a while. You might be able to go through the cycle again within a few minutes or short-cut the cycle and go from explosion to tension-building to explosion without the other phases.

Grief and remorse

You might feel guilt after seeing the amount of pain you have inflicted. You might feel sadness for others whom you hurt. You might be embarrassed to realize how out of control you were, especially if you pride yourself on being in control. Or you may not experience this phase. You may even feel justified for the torment you inflicted. You need to ask yourself if you are truly remorseful and want to change. You might be manipulating the victim because you are afraid of her leaving you. If you are not sorry and at the same time making promises to change and finding ways to blame the victim, your tension is building.

Martin said he felt terrible about what happened and that he was going to have to find a way to make it up to his wife, but he insisted she should have come home after work. He rationalized by explaining that if she had not gone to the mall, then he would not have had to worry about her.

Change is the Third Path
M. Lindsey, R. McBride and C. Platt

The Cycle of Violence

(Adapted from Lenore Walker, The Battered Woman, 1979.)

Shouting
Shoving
Grabbing
Breaking furniture
Punching walls
Hurting pets
Slapping
Choking
Punching
Sexual attacks
Stabbing
Shooting

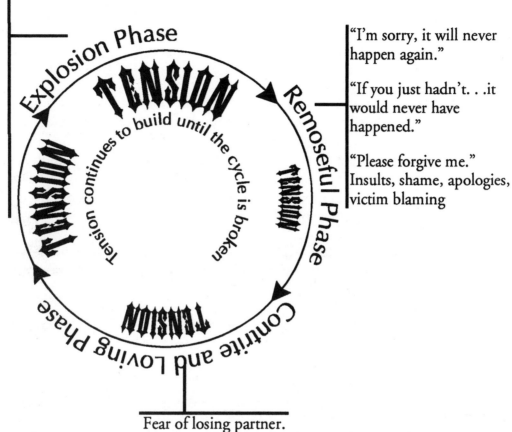

"I'm sorry, it will never happen again."

"If you just hadn't. . .it would never have happened."

"Please forgive me." Insults, shame, apologies, victim blaming

Fear of losing partner.
"I'd do anything to get her back."
Dutiful lover, unusually passionate.
Buying presents, overly considerate, concerned, resentful

The tension is not dissipated by the explosion. It never stops building until the cycle is broken because:
you have stress and unresolved conflict
you are feeling humiliated, inadequate, threatened, intimidated
you have guilt over the explosion
you fear losing your partner and will say anything to keep from leaving
you don't believe you were wrong
you feel demeaned having to make-up or apologize

As the cycle repeats, the violence usually becomes more frequent and more severe.
The remorseful and contrite stages may disappear.
The cycle may take minutes or months.

Contrite phase—hearts and flowers

Is this you? Once the tension is relieved you are often able to realize you have misdirected the anger and that the content of your attack was irrational. After feeling guilty and remorseful, you ask for an opportunity to make amends.

Fearing that your mate may leave, you "do anything" to get back with your partner. You become a dutiful lover, helpful, passive and contrite. You buy her presents, become overly concerned and considerate, and atypically passionate during this phase.

Your passivity and attentiveness also become the groundwork for building tension, as you think or say: "Look at all I've done and she still is not satisfied. What do I have to do for her to forgive me?" You are minimizing your partner's fear and expect that forgiveness "should" be given once you have apologized for your behavior. Are you now feeling controlled by her, unable to escape, powerless and trapped? You are in fact trapped not by her, but by your own fears, beliefs and dependency needs. Your tension continues to build.

> Discuss with the group the phase you are in and how that feels. If you are living with your partner, discuss the cycle of violence as it relates to your relationship.
>
> Learning the cycle is a good tool to help you end your abuse and violence and gain confidence.

It is important to identity where you are in the cycle of violence at any given time. Practice by sitting down several times a day to check in with yourself. If you are building toward an explosion, stop and devise a plan. If you build tension and rage rapidly, learn to identify the early warning signs and force yourself to use a Time Out (see page 68).

Change is the Third Path
M. Lindsey, R. McBride and C. Platt

What Are My External Stressors?

Money: (For example: I don't make enough.) _____
_____
_____

Competition/shame: (For example: My kids are dressed more poorly than the neighbors' kids.) _____
_____
_____

Criticism: (For example: People always know what's best for me.) _____
_____
_____

Family: (For example: If I can't succeed in my life, how can I be successful with a family?) _____
_____
_____

Write down other areas that create stress for you:

1. _____
_____

2. _____
_____

3. _____
_____

4. _____
_____

5. _____
_____
_____

Adapted from Rob Gallup

Time Out

A Tool To Stop Your Abuse And Violence

✔ Violence is a choice.

✔ You must discuss, agree, and practice the Time Out with your partner, so your partner knows what you are doing.

✔ Time Out is not a solution but it will help until you get to the root of the problem.

Recognize Your Anger

Monitor Your Conflict—Be aware when you are no longer engaged in constructive arguing.

Monitor Your Body Signs—Racing thoughts, inability to listen, flushed face, headache, pounding heart, sweating palms, tense jaws and clenched fists.

Monitor Your Self Talk—Listen to what you are telling yourself. Are you saying negative things about yourself, your partner or the situation? This escalates the anger. Are you name-calling, cursing, and giving commands such as, "Get off my back" or "I told you to shut up?" Violent language also escalates your anger.

Take A Time Out

Tell your partner you are taking a Time Out.
Do not second guess yourself.
Do not get the last word in.
Simply say, "I am taking a Time Out" and leave.

Leave For One Hour

Don't drink or drug. Don't drive.
Don't hit pillows, walls, or a punching bag. (These are rehearsal for violent actions.)
Do something physical, such as walking, running, bicycling, lifting weights.
Do relaxation techniques, such as deep breathing.
Do positive self-talk, "I am taking responsibility for myself," "I didn't strike out at anyone," "I am a good person," "I will be okay."
Check out your feelings, using "I" statements, "I feel hurt," "I feel sad," or "I feel embarrassed."
Check out what you think your partner's point of view might be.

Check Back In

Once your anger is under control and you want to talk with your mate, ask if now is a good time to talk. If she is still angry, wait. If she is willing to talk, explain why you felt angry. Attempt to resolve the conflict. If you cannot resolve the conflict, table it for another time and follow through later. If the conversation leads to escalation of the anger, stop and repeat the Time Out process.

LOOK FOR WIN/WIN SOLUTIONS. A resolution must be acceptable to both parties for it to work.

Change is the Third Path
M. Lindsey, R. McBride and C. Platt

Time Out Worksheet

Make several copies of this worksheet. Use it when you take a Time Out. It will help give you some direction during your Time Out and help you analyze why you are taking a Time Out.

Define the Problem

I believe the problem is:

I feel_____about_____

I feel_____about _____

I feel_____about _____

My perception is that:

She feels_____about _____

She feels_____about _____

She feels_____about _____

Self-Talk

What am I telling myself about the situation?_____

_____

What am I telling myself about my partner? _____

_____

What are some things I can tell myself to help me calm down (Positive Self-Talk)? _____

Tension Cues

Recognizing feelings is an essential skill you need to develop so that you can end your abusive and violent behavior. The ability to understand feelings begins by paying attention to sensations within your body. These sensations are cues that you are building tension and they can act as early warning signs that you are going to have an angry outburst or be violent.

Circle the tension cues which you experienced and *warned* you to take a Time Out:

Nervous sweat	Anxious feeling
Increased heart rate	Sweaty palms
Headache	Irritable feeling
Tense muscles	Heartburn
Facial tension	Uptight feeling
Other (specify)_____	

Problem Solving

List three possible solutions to the problem (look for Win/Win solutions).

1. _____

2. _____

3. _____

Understanding My Jealousy and Obsession

Jealousy is a complex feeling because attached to or underlying it can be many other feelings. Essentially feelings of jealousy fall into two broad categories—rational and irrational.

Rational Jealousy

Rational jealousy may occur when your significant other gets involved with other people or activities that take attention, care, affection, or time away from you. Your response to this might be anger, resentment, fear, attempts to manipulate, coercion, or violence. These responses are not productive to any relationship because they do not create increased closeness but serve to drive your mate away.

An effective response requires that you first examine your role in the process and relationship.

Have I asked for what I want?   ☐ Yes   ☐ No
If no, why not?_____

Am I afraid to ask for what I want?   ☐ Yes   ☐ No
If yes, why?_____

Do I know what I want?   ☐ Yes   ☐ No

If yes, did I ask for the right thing?   ☐ Yes   ☐ No
If no, why not?_____

Is it reasonable to get what I want?   ☐ Yes   ☐ No

Can my mate give me what I want?   ☐ Yes   ☐ No

Am I doing my part in the relationship?   ☐ Yes   ☐ No
If no, why not?_____

Change is the Third Path
M. Lindsey, R. McBride and C. Platt

Do I ignore my relationship by being overly involved in:

☐ Work activities   ☐ Sports or entertainment activities
☐ A never ending list of projects around the home
☐ No

Am I involved in alcohol or drugs?   ☐ Yes   ☐ No
Am I isolated?   ☐ Yes   ☐ No

I trust people.   ☐ Yes   ☐ No
If no, why not?_____

I am trying to draw her into my isolation. ☐ Yes   ☐ No

She has invited me to join in her world but I have refused.
                                       ☐ Yes   ☐ No
If I have refused, why?_____

Ultimately, even when jealousy is rational you will need to examine, understand, and control the feelings that co-exist with the jealousy. Can you identify with the following feelings?

I fear being abandoned by my partner. ☐ Yes   ☐ No
If yes, why?_____

I sense that my special position is threatened.☐ Yes   ☐ No
If yes, why?_____

I feel inadequate.   ☐ Yes   ☐ No
If yes, why?_____

Ending rational jealousy requires that you take responsibility for your feelings and choices rather than blaming your mate and demanding that she change. This means having many conversations about both of your positions and feelings. Conversations in which positions are negotiated, compromises and agreements are made and feelings acknowledged and validated. You should take special care not to let this dialog become an extension of badgering or harassment designed to pressure your mate to change.

Irrational Jealousy

Irrational jealousy occurs when you *believe*, *perceive*, or *feel* that your mate is involved with other people or activities that take attention, care, affection, or time away from you. Unlike rational jealousy there is no truth to these beliefs or perceptions.

Three of the most common "themes" involved in irrational jealousy are:
My mate is having an affair.
My mate spends more time with her family than me.
My mate is more involved with her work and friends than me.

People who experience jealousy which is not founded in reality do so for a variety of reasons. Can you identify with any of the follow reasons.

I feel inadequate—I'm not handsome, smart, or emotional enough or cannot provide enough.

I am thinking about or am having an affair and imagine my mate must also be having an affair.

I am frightened by women's sexuality and believe women cannot control themselves sexually. I see women either as virgins or whores.

I am isolated—the only person involved with me is my mate. (Refer to the diagram on page 99.)

In either case the most severe jealousy involves obsession. Constant intrusive thoughts concerning your partner or ex-partner (target) with intense desire or need to act on the thoughts in an effort to fix your feelings of abandonment, betrayal, or injury to self-worth.

Obsession

A most difficult and potentially destructive aspect of abusive and violent relationships is the overwhelming feelings that create an intense need for control. These tremendous feelings of fear, betrayal, anger, loss, and abandonment can result from a variety of imagined or real situations.

Examples of imagined situations are:
My mate may leave me.
My mate may have an affair.

This type of thinking creates great distress for many individuals. The goal of their behavior becomes an attempt to avoid the loss of a mate or to stop her from having an affair. Two strategies to control the feelings attached to the thoughts are often employed by these individuals. One strategy is to direct efforts toward controlling the victim through control of money, time, access to friends and family, and use of coercion, threats, emotional abuse, and repeated asking for reassurance. For a more complete list of these tactic review page 13.

The other strategy attempts to reduce the distress through "thinking" about the problem or "planning" about what to do about the problem. Obsessed persons gather information through indirect and direct means by spying, interrogating the woman and children, talking to friends and family, reading private letters and journals, going through trash. By repeatedly thinking about the problem and the possible solutions, obsessive individuals act as if this *pretend* method for gaining control is taking action.

Change is the Third Path
M. Lindsey, R. McBride and C. Platt

Both strategies are doomed to failure because the real problem resides within the abusive and violent individuals. It is their fear of loss that must be confronted.

Examples of fears based in reality are:
My mate is leaving or she has left me.
My mate is having or has had an affair.

When reality involves a separation or a mate having an affair, the pain and disruption to normal routine can be so great that people can become partially or totally immobilized. They may find their ability to focus on work impaired and may not be able to eat or sleep.

Obsessive individuals may focus on getting their mate to return to the marriage or they may decided to punish her. In the event of a separation or an affair these individuals often find themselves feeling not only betrayed but as if everything of value has been taken from them. They feel empty as though there is no sense of self. In an effort to reconstruct some form of life, obsessive individuals become focused on their mate. In the worst cases obsessive individuals become totally focused on the "plan" to the exclusion of all other aspects of life. They may:

Try to force her to return by harassing her by phone or in person, threatening to take the children, and threatening to destroy her reputation, harm her property, damage her employment.

Try to prove to the world she is the bad person and he is the good person in the relationship. They make attacks on the character of the victim and recriminations about their victimization.

Review the *Obsession Checklist* below to see if any of the items on the list apply to you.

Obsession Checklist

☐ I've had suicidal thoughts/attempts ☐ I've had homicidal thoughts/attempts

☐ I am not eating ☐ I am not sleeping

☐ I am not working ☐ I have no activities

☐ I am isolated ☐ I am depressed

☐ In therapy, I focus on the target.

☐ In therapy, I focus on plans for reconciliation.

☐ I have intrusive thoughts. For example: she is having sex with others.

☐ I make repeated attempts to contact victim.

☐ I focus on plans for reattachment, vindication, or revenge.

☐ I have a hard time thinking or solving problems.

☐ I am unable to acknowledge my choices or options—rigid.

☐ I am unable to stop my feelings of emotional injury.

☐ I have profound feelings of betrayal, abandonment, or annihilation.

☐ I have a short-view time frame for my future.

If you have not read the section Batterers Who Stalk, page 17, read it now. Then review the *Stalking Behavior Checklist* on, page 19, to see if you are involved in any of those behaviors.

Stalking Behavior Present: ☐ Yes   ☐ No

If you are in this situation and involved in these kinds of behaviors, regardless of the pain, your goal must change. Your significant other may have created conflict and even pain but your method of solving it is unacceptable. Your strategies for ending your pain are wrong, criminal, destructive, dangerous and doomed to fail. This is not the way to handled the situation and the results of your behavior will achieve the opposite of what you want. There is another way to live your life where you can achieve a sense of well-being. You must begin by working with your therapist on the following areas.

Your isolation must end. Perhaps you can connect with other men in your group or join in the activities of an appropriate social, recreational or spiritual organization.

It is necessary that you find and maintain productive activity such as a job.

It is essential for you to continue functioning in your daily routine of working, eating, sleeping, and recreation while you try to understand and work through your feelings of loss, fear, betrayal, etc.

All of your attempts to control the other person must end. You can never control anyone else's thoughts, feelings, or actions, you can only control your thoughts, feelings, or actions. If you try to do otherwise, you will become frustrated.

Develop a strategy for the creation of a new life with or without your mate. Start by ending behaviors that cause your mate and children to fear you. Also, begin to eliminate the chaos you have created in your life. It is entirely your choice and responsibility whether you have a meaningful or meaningless life.

Understanding My Anger

Abuse and violence are not about your anger. They are about control and your feelings of hurt, fear, humiliation, guilt, loss and threat. These feelings may give rise to anger, then rage, then abuse. Anger and rage are safer for most men than expressing feelings that involve vulnerability. The following exercises are intended to help you understand and control your anger and rage. They will help you begin to identify and understand the feelings you have that are covered up by the anger and rage.

Anger is an emotional reaction to stressors and can have positive results; however, you escalate your anger to a point where the results are negative.

Anger

+ Positive
✔ An energizer
✔ A way to express tension
✔ A cure for some problems

– Negative
✔ When it creates fatigue and weakness
✔ When it pushes people away
✔ When it is too frequent
✔ When it is too intense
✔ When it lasts too long
✔ When it leads to aggression
✔ When it disturbs work
✔ When it controls the relationship

Useful
✔ Self-enhancing
✔ Productive
✔ Adaptive

Useless
✔ Self-destructive
✔ Non-productive
✔ Maladaptive

How does my anger work for me in positive ways? _____

_____

How does my anger work work against me in negative ways? _____

_____

Language of Hate

The ability to dehumanize increases the chance for violence to occur because it is easier to hurt objects rather than people. It is clear in war that the enemy is given ugly non-human qualities and re-labeled as less than human. Everyday many people use the language of hate when they are feeling threatened, angry, and enraged. They use it in reference to or toward strangers, casual acquaintances, co-workers, friends, and loved ones. People use this language of hate to threaten and control others because they don't know how or are afraid to express how they feel about a situation.

You are not likely to get sympathy, support, or understanding when you use the language of hate. You are most likely to get fear, anger and hate in return. It is difficult if not impossible for others to understand how you feel because you are not communicating feelings when you use the language of hate.

When you corrupt sexuality with the language of hate, you dehumanize a person toward whom you have sexual, i.e. intimate feelings. Dehumanization enables you to be abusive. As you define each word below ask yourself what affect the image created has on your relationship with your partner.

In this exercise the words commonly have two meanings. Write both meanings then discuss what you have concluded about the language of hate as it pertains to men and women. For example, is it good or bad to be fucked?

Fucked _____

_____

Screwed _____

_____

Pussy _____

_____

Cunt _____

_____

Cocksucker _____

_____

Bitch _____

_____

What other words can you add to the language of hate?
Do you use hateful language? *How does this language reflect your attitudes toward women?*

The Anger Elevator

Adapted from "The Anger Elevator" by Gary McCune

Out of Control	10	Words	Thoughts	Body Signals	Behaviors
High Levels	9	enraged	Thoughts are directed with intention of taking action— controlling, stopping or punishing.	Clinched fist	Hitting
	8	furious		Shouting, talking fast	Shouting
	7	ticked off	Thoughts of telling spouse off		Grabbing
	6	angry	Thoughts that are more directed toward the person or object.	Veins popped out	
Middle Levels	5	mad		Tight jaw	Slamming objects
	4	agitated	"She should be home by now!"	Flushed face	Pacing
	3	irritated	"Where is she?"	Wrinkled brow	Obsessing
	2	annoyed	"I wonder why he or she is not home yet?"	Tight muscles	Observing and thinking
Low Levels	1	bothered	Awareness, something is not right.	Mild tension arousal	
				Not noticeable	Goes about activities

The Anger Elevator Exercise

Go back over the last episode of violence. In each of the columns below—Thought, Body Signals, Behaviors— at each level of anger write on the top line what happened during the episode. On the next line, write what you could have done differently at each step.

Out of Control		Words	Thoughts	Body Signals	Behaviors
High Levels	10				
		enraged	_____	_____	_____
	9		_____	_____	_____
			_____	_____	_____
	8	furious	_____	_____	_____
			_____	_____	_____
	7		_____	_____	_____
		ticked off	_____	_____	_____
	6	angry	_____	_____	_____
Middle Levels			_____	_____	_____
	5	mad	_____	_____	_____
			_____	_____	_____
	4	agitated	_____	_____	_____
			_____	_____	_____
	3	irritated	_____	_____	_____
			_____	_____	_____
	2	annoyed	_____	_____	_____
			_____	_____	_____
Low Levels	1	bothered	_____	_____	_____

Change is the Third Path
M. Lindsey, R. McBride and C. Platt

Four Ways to Express My Anger

I can stuff it (give an example).

When have I said it doesn't matter?

_____

When have I denied it happened?

_____

When have I felt bad without expressing it?

_____

When have I felt humiliated?

_____

I can handle it indirectly (give an example).

How have I been indirectly critical?

_____

How have I been sarcastic?

_____

How have I found ways to pay back without being caught?

_____

I can escalate it (give an example).

How have I continuously reviewed grievances?

_____

How have I continuously blamed others?

_____

How have I justified revenge?

_____

How have I used punishment?

_____

How have I used violence?

_____

Leads to destruction of relationships and usually to prison.

I can handle it directly (give an example).

When have I been specific about my anger?

_____

When have I expressed my anger without threats or escalation?

_____

When have I taken responsibility for my anger?

_____

When have I asked a person to change or stop the behavior?

_____

How do I express my anger?

_____

_____

Do I express my anger differently with different people? Explain.

_____

_____

Which methods of expressing anger work best for me? _____

_____

_____

The process of getting to the feelings your anger covers up is simple.

✔ You must begin by slowing down. This means stop reacting immediately to all the situations you perceive as problems.

✔ As you slow down, pay attention to your physical sensations—heat, chill, rushing, tingling, pressure. . . .

✔ Think about these sensations.

✔ Pay attention to your actions—quiet pacing, clenched teeth, clenched fists, yelling, punching the wall. . . .

✔ Think about your actions.

✔ If your anger is developing, look beneath it for other feelings.

✔ Look at the list of feelings on page 95. What feelings apply?

✔ Talk about those feelings.

Discovering what feelings lie beneath your anger is one reason for using Time Outs.

A good way to explore your anger and the feelings behind it is to keep a simple journal. Get a notebook or start by using the Anger Journal on the next page and keep track of how many times a day or week you get angry. What time was it? Where were you? Write down the sensations and feelings you experienced. Also, write about how you reacted or the action you took to resolve you anger. Study the examples as a start then start your own journal.

Anger Journal

Date & Time	Place	Perceived Problem	Sensations	Feelings	Actions
June 7-8 p.m.	Home	Janet wants more money for bills	pressure, hot	guilty, defensive	yelled, swore
June 10-9:30 a.m.	Work	Boss said I didn't work hard enough	tight jaw, stomach	angry, wronged	stuffed it
June 11-2 a.m.	Bedrm.	Couldn't sleep/thinking about work.	mind spinning	mad, worried	went for a walk

My History of Anger and Violence

Men who are abusive and violent like to believe each episode of violence and abuse is a separate event that they can explain. The events are not separate. They are a pattern of behavior which affects everyone involved.

Recording the history of your violence will help you understand two things—where you learned to be violent and why your mate is afraid and angry.

Doing this exercise honestly is emotionally painful. Abuse and violence take an emotional and physical toll. Awareness of the pain involved can help you stop your abusive and violent behavior. Reconstruct how your family members dealt with anger and how it affected each of them.

Write about two times when your father was angry. _____
_____
_____

When your father was angry, how did your mother look and act?
_____
_____

How did the kids look and act? _____
_____
_____

How did you feel about your father's anger? _____
_____
_____

Write about two times when your mother was angry. _____
_____
_____

When your mother was angry, how did your father look and act?
_____
_____

How did the kids look and act? _____
_____
_____

How did you feel about your mother's anger? _____
_____
_____

Change is the Third Path
M. Lindsey, R. McBride and C. Platt

Write about two times when your stepfather/foster father was angry.

_____

_____

When your stepfather/foster father was angry, how did your mother/foster mother look and act? _____

_____

How did the children look and act? _____

_____

_____

How did you feel about your stepfather/foster father's anger?

_____

_____

Write about two times when your stepmother/foster mother was angry.

_____

_____

When your stepmother/foster mother was angry, how did your father/foster father look and act? _____

_____

How did the children look and act?

_____

_____

How did you feel about your stepmother/foster mother's anger?

_____

_____

Write about the first time you were angry. _____

_____

_____

When was the first time you hit someone? How did it feel?

_____

_____

What happened next? _____

_____

_____

When was the first time you were hit? How did it feel?

_____

_____

What happened next?_____

_____

Write about two times you were angry and abusive to your partner.

_____

_____

How did your partner look and act? _____

_____

_____

How did your children look and act? _____

_____

_____

When was the first time you hit your mate. How did it feel?

_____

_____

How did your partner look and act? _____

_____

_____

How did your children look and act? _____

_____

_____

What happened next?_____

_____

_____

_____

_____

Bible Verses Regarding Anger

Adapted from Gary McCune

Often abusive and violent men misquote and misinterpret the Bible to dominate their mates and justify their behavior. The following Bible quotations refute their position or excuses.

Psalms 37:8 Refrain from anger and turn from wrath; do not fret. It leads only to evil.

Proverbs 5:21 For a man's ways are in full view of the Lord, and he examines all his paths.

14:17 A quick-tempered man does foolish things, and a crafty man is hated.

14:29 A patient man has great understanding, but a quick-tempered man displays folly.

15:1 A gentle answer turns away wrath, but a harsh word stirs up anger.

15:18 A hot-tempered man stirs up dissension, but a patient man calms a quarrel.

16:29 A violent man entices his neighbor and leads him down a path that is not good.

16:32 Better a patient man than a warrior, a man who controls his temper than one who takes a city.

19:19 A hot-tempered man must pay the penalty; if you rescue him, you will have to do it again.

22:24-25 Do not make friends with a hot-tempered man, do not associate with one easily angered, or you may learn his ways and get yourself ensnared.

25:28 Like a city whose walls are broken down is a man who lacks self-control.

28:13 He who conceals his sins does not prosper, but whoever confesses and renounces them finds mercy.

29:11 A fool gives full vent to his anger, but a wise man keeps himself under control.

29:22 An angry man stirs up dissension, and a hot-tempered one commits many sins.

Ecclesiastes 7: 9 Do not be quickly provoked in your spirit, for anger resides in the lap of fools.

	8:11 When the sentence for a crime is not quickly carried out, the hearts of the people are filled with schemes to do wrong.
Ephesians	4:26,27 In your anger do not sin: Do not let the sun go down while you are still angry, and do not give the devil a foothold.
Colossians	3: 8 But now you must rid yourselves of all such things as these: anger, rage, malice, slander, filthy language.
Titus	1:7 Since an overseer is entrusted with God's work, he must be blameless, not overbearing, not quick-tempered, not given to much wine, not violent, not pursuing dishonest gain.
James	1:19 My dear brothers, take note of this: Everyone should be quick to listen, slow to speak, and slow to become angry.

Bible Verses Regarding Time Outs

Proverbs	17:14 Starting a quarrel is like breaching a dam; so drop the matter before a dispute breaks out.
	19:11 A man's wisdom gives him patience; it is to his glory to overlook an offense.
	20:3 It is to a man's honor to avoid strife, but every fool is quick to quarrel.
	20:22 Do not say, "I'll pay you back for this wrong!" Wait for the Lord, and he will deliver you.
	21:23 He who guards his mouth and his tongue keeps himself from calamity.

How To Resolve My Anger

Learn to keep my anger at a moderate level.

Learn to understand feelings and express them appropriately (see page 95).

Learn to understand other people's feelings.

Learn to stop blaming others for my anger.

Learn problem solving skills (see page 108).

Learn to use assertiveness skills (see page 104).

Learn to communicate without using threats (see page 112).

Learn to use relaxation skills (see page 116).

Family of Origin

Families provide children with basic knowledge about different aspects of life. They model conflict resolution and role expectations for men and women. In addition, families teach values, provide safety or instill terror and they establish the mechanism for forming meaningful and healthy attachments or alienation.

The list of good and bad traits that families can model for their members is lengthy. By reflecting on and examining your family experience, you can see what you were taught. From the awareness you gain, you can begin to alter your attitudes, values and old patterns of destructive behavior. Long established, destructive elements of behavior that have been passed down to you can be replaced with new constructive behaviors and habits that will enhance your life.

Your therapist can help you analyze information about your family and assist you in finding alternative information about families.

History and Family of Origin

On the time line, write significant events in your life and the age at which they occurred. For example: parents' divorce, emotional or physical or sexual abuse, deaths, marriage, estrangement.

Birth   Today

Describe the members of your family and how each affected the significant events of your life.

Father _____

_____

_____

Mother_____
_____
_____

Stepfather_____
_____
_____

Stepmother _____
_____
_____

Brothers (including step siblings) _____
_____
_____

Sisters (including step siblings) _____
_____
_____

Grandparents _____
_____

Any other significant people (aunts, uncles, foster parents, teachers, friends)
_____
_____
_____

What was my role in the family? _____
_____
_____

How did I relate to other members of my family?_____
_____
_____
_____

What were the roles of each member of my family?
_____
_____
_____

Who was the "boss" in my family and how did I know this? _____
_____

Who got along best and who had the most conflict? _____
_____
_____

Change is the Third Path
M. Lindsey, R. McBride and C. Platt

How was conflict dealt with in my family? _____
_____

What were the important rules in my family? _____
_____
_____
_____

Which were the "unspoken" rules? _____
_____
_____

How was discipline dealt with in my family? _____
_____
_____

Who got in the most trouble? _____
_____

Who did what kinds of discipline? _____
_____
_____

Was I physically, sexually or emotionally abused? _____
_____

Any other thoughts I have about my family of origin?_____
_____
_____

Have you considered writing a letter to any members of your family with which you have unfinished business, unexpressed feelings or grievances? Writing a letter to them can help clarify the issues you have with them and help you look at your unresolved feelings. (It does not matter if they are alive or not, or whether or not you mail the letter. Talk to your therapist about this idea.)

If you were to write a letter to a relative, what are some of your thoughts you would like to express?

_____
_____
_____
_____
_____
_____
_____
_____
_____

Control

People use different types of behavior attempting to exercise control over others—passive, passive-aggressive, and aggressive. Being overly agreeable, emotionally dishonest, indirect, self-denying are means of attempting to passively control others. Passive people give mates, children, friends and others money, gifts, time, and feelings in an effort to be liked or loved, avoid anger or punishment and stop loss or abandonment. They sacrifice because of their beliefs about themselves—they feel inadequate, worthless, unimportant, vulnerable. Although they try to show a healthy facade, they are driven by the fear that others will discover the truth. They keep giving trying to indirectly get something in return—happiness, love, satisfaction— until they become resentful and angry.

Overly agreeable, emotional dishonesty, indirectness, and self-denying are also part of the attempt to control others passive-aggressively. Passive-aggressive people often believe they cannot trust anyone and must outsmart others to get their needs met. When their mate disagrees with them, they withdraw love or support to punish her. They agree to do something then don't do it. They agree to more than they want then blame others for asking too much.

Aggressive people attempt to control other people by being inappropriately honest, direct, attacking, blaming. They believe they are entitled to what they want, must look out for themselves and are the center of the universe. While they present themselves differently, they hold similar beliefs as passive persons—they feel inadequate, worthless, unimportant, vulnerable.

Some people try to gain power and can get what they want by controlling other people. In relationships, people do not gain power or get what they want in the long-run by dominating another—passively or aggressively. Power is the ability or capacity to act or perform effectively as a human being in controlling our thoughts, feelings, and actions. Equality and sharing are the ingredients in a relationship that will help us find what we want.

As we said earlier, it is healthy to establish reasonable boundaries and limits for ourselves and to exercise control over our lives. However, the difference between you and other men is that you have carried control to an extreme. You have an excessive need to gain and maintain control not only over your life but also the lives of others. You probably try to manage one situation after another in an attempt to maximize your control. This level of control is impossible to attain and leads to continuous conflict that frustrates and exhausts you.

You made a choice to use abuse and violence as a means of resolving conflict when you are hurt, frightened, threatened, attacked, feeling guilty or failing. You may believe your behavior is not manipulating, intimidating, or controlling or you may believe threats and force are necessary to handle the situation. You may feel totally justified in the use of force because you want your mate to stop a specific behavior, to do something different, or you want to punish her. Your violence is designed to control a given situation and it often works in the short run. In the long run, your violence only serves to destroy you and the ones you love.

You do not realize the paradox:
The more you try to control, the less control you have.

The next three exercises can help you decide whether or not equality exists in your relationship.

Control

Social

I isolate her and control what she does, who she sees and talks to, what she reads, where she goes. I try to limit her outside involvement and use jealousy to justify my actions.

☐ Never   ☐ Sometimes   ☐ Often

Emotional

I put her down, criticize, humiliate and/or call her names. I make her feel bad about herself, think she's crazy, and feel guilty.

☐ Never   ☐ Sometimes   ☐ Often

Economic

I prevent her from getting and keeping a job. I make her ask for money, and/or take her money. I do not allow her to know about or have access to the family income.

☐ Never   ☐ Sometimes   ☐ Often

Sexual

I force sex against her will. I force her to do sexual things with which she feels uncomfortable.

☐ Never   ☐ Sometimes   ☐ Often

Children

I use guilt about the children and use our children to hurt her. I use visitations to harass her. I threaten to take the children from her.

☐ Never   ☐ Sometimes   ☐ Often

Intimidation and Threats	I intimidate her with looks, actions, gestures, and a loud voice. I threaten to leave her, hurt her, commit suicide, or kidnap the children to get my way. I destroy our property and display weapons.
	☐ Never ☐ Sometimes ☐ Often
Male Privilege	I treat her like a servant and act like master of the household. I make all the major decisions.
	☐ Never ☐ Sometimes ☐ Often

Equality

Developing a relationship based on equality has benefits for everyone. Each person in a relationship can use their strengths to help solve problems, which makes life easier. Closeness is enhanced when each person feels safe and empowered to speak or act as a respected adult.

Social	I encourage her in social relations by supporting her goals in life and respecting her right to her own feelings, friends, activities, and opinions.
	☐ Never ☐ Sometimes ☐ Often
Emotional	I listen to her non-judgementally and value her opinions. I am emotionally affirming and understanding.
	☐ Never ☐ Sometimes ☐ Often
Economic	I support her work and we mutually decide how the money is spent. Both partners benefit from the financial arrangement.
	☐ Never ☐ Sometimes ☐ Often
Sexual	Sex is by mutual consent. I am interested in and understanding of her feelings and needs.
	☐ Never ☐ Sometimes ☐ Often
Children	I deal directly with my partner, not through the children. I share parental responsibilities and present a positive non-violent role model for the children.
	☐ Never ☐ Sometimes ☐ Often
Non-threatening	I talk and act so that she feels safe and comfortable expressing herself and doing things. I negotiate my needs, and seek a mutually satisfying resolution to conflict.
	☐ Never ☐ Sometimes ☐ Often
Shared responsibility	We mutually agree on a fair distribution of work and family decisions. We share responsibility.
	☐ Never ☐ Sometimes ☐ Often

Three Things I Can Control

People have the capacity to act on their environment in order to improve, change or direct future possibilities. This capacity to control is a wonderful tool when used appropriately. Unfortunately most people react to feelings of fear or powerlessness with an increased effort to control events or people when control is not possible. This is especially true for individuals who are abusive or violent.

The only things you can control are: your thoughts, your feelings and your behaviors. When you try to control anything else, you are doomed to failure and your level of fear and powerlessness increases. Paradoxically when you focus on the power associated with controlling yourself, your fear and powerlessness diminish. The exercises on *Control* and *Equality* and this exercise will help you begin to focus on some of the behaviors you need to examine and change.

List three of my mate's behaviors I try to control.

1. _____
2. _____
3. _____

How do I try to control them? _____
_____
_____

How do I feel if I fail to control her behavior? _____
_____
_____

List three other things in my life I try to control.

1. _____
2. _____
3. _____

How do I try to control them? _____
_____
_____
_____

How do I feel if I fail to control them? _____
_____
_____

Three Things I Can Control: My Feelings, My Thoughts, My Behaviors.
Trying to control others' thoughts, feelings and behaviors is futile because people struggle against being controlled. Your attempt to control others creates frustration, feelings of powerlessness, fear and anger for you.

How Do I Feel?

Many men are taught that feelings are better left unexpressed. They may learn that expressing feelings is a sign of weakness and will leave them vulnerable to attack. When you grow up believing that it's dangerous or unmanly to express feelings other than anger, anger is one of the few feelings you'll be aware of. It becomes your all-purpose response.

As an abusive and violent man you are likely to be less in touch with your feelings than most men. You have shut off your internal world because it was too painful and confusing as a child. You probably cannot tolerate strong feelings, particularly hurt, loss, fear, sadness and powerlessness. You probably rely heavily on the traditional male role because it helps you stifle your real feelings.

As an abusive and violent man, you have learned to block your emotional pain by ignoring it or pushing it aside and going to anger-rage-violence. You can often express thoughts but you have great difficulty expressing your feelings. As long as you cannot allow yourself to feel sadness, hurt, fear of abandonment, guilt, embarrassment, weakness and loss you will be at risk of being violent.

Men often think that showing anger, rage, jealousy and saying "fuck you" are safe ways of expressing their feelings. If this is the way you express yourself, you are actually repressing your feelings and people become confused when they cannot understand how you feel.

A common example is of two men in conflict on the street, at work or in recreation: A situation occurs between them and one man says, "Fuck you!" The other man replies with, "Fuck you, too, asshole!" The first man responds with, "Fuck your mother, you cocksucker!" The exchange goes on until one person hits, stabs or shoots the other. What if the first man had said, "Don't do that. It hurts my feelings," and the second man replied, "I'm sorry." Does this sound silly to you? It does to most men yet hundreds of thousands of friendships are broken, thousands of men die and thousands of men go to prison because they are unable or unwilling to express feelings other than rage.

Change is the Third Path
M. Lindsey, R. McBride and C. Platt

The Alphabet of Feelings

Knowing how you feel is a start on the path of recovery
These are feelings people have but often fail to identify

A

ABANDONED
ADEQUATE
ADAMANT
AFFECTIONATE
AGONIZED
AMBIVALENT
AMOROUS
AMUSED
ANGRY
ANNOYED
ANXIOUS
APATHETIC
AWARE
AWED

B

BAD
BEAUTIFUL
BETRAYED
BITTER
BLISSFUL
BOLD
BORED
BRAVE
BURDENED

C

CALM
CAPABLE
CAPTIVATED
CHALLENGED
CHEATED
CHEERFUL
CHILDISH
CLEVER
COMBATIVE
CONDEMNED
CONFUSED
CONSPICUOUS
CONTENTED
CONTRITE
CRUEL
CRUSHED
CULPABLE

D

DECEITFUL
DEFEATED
DELIGHTED
DEPRESSED
DESIROUS
DESPAIRING
DESTRUCTIVE
DETERMINED
DIFFERENT
DIFFIDENT
DIMINISHED
DISCONTENTED
DISTRACTED
DISTRAUGHT
DISTRUSTFUL
DISTURBED
DOMINATED
DIVIDED
DRIVEN
DUBIOUS

E

EAGER
ECSTATIC
EMPTY
ENCHANTED
ENERGETIC
ENERVATED
ENVIOUS
EXCITED
EVIL
EXASPERATED
EXHAUSTED
EXHILARATED

F

FASCINATED
FAWNING
FEARFUL
FLUSTERED
FOOLISH
FRANTIC
FRUSTRATED
FRIGHTENED
FREE
FULL
FUNNY
FURIOUS

G

GAY
GLAD
GLAMOROUS
GOOD
GRATIFIED
GREEDY
GRIEVED
GUILTY
GULLIBLE

H

HAPPY
HATEFUL
HELPFUL
HELPLESS
HIGH
HOMESICK
HONORED
HORRIBLE
HURT
HYSTERICAL

I

IGNORED
IMMORAL
IMMORTAL
IMPOSED UPON
IMPRESSED
INADEQUATE
INFATUATED
INFURIATED
INSPIRED
INTIMIDATED
ISOLATED

J

JADED
JEALOUS
JOYOUS
JUMPY

K

KIND
KEEN

L

LACONIC
LAZY
LECHEROUS
LEFT OUT
LICENTIOUS
LONELY
LONGING
LOVING
LOW
LUSTFUL

M

MAD
MAUDLIN
MEAN
MELANCHOLY
MISERABLE
MYSTICAL

N

NAUGHTY
NAUSEATED
NEAT
NERVOUS
NICE
NIGGARDLY
NUTTY

O

OBNOXIOUS
OBSESSED
ODD
OPPRESSED
OUTRAGED
OVERWHELMED

P

PAINED
PANICKED
PARSIMONIOUS
PEACEFUL
PERSECUTED
PETRIFIED
PITIFUL
PITEOUS
PLEASANT
PLEASED
PRECARIOUS
PRESSURED
PRETTY
PRIM
PRISSY
PROUD

Q

QUARRELSOME
QUEER

R

RAGEFUL
RAPTUROUS
REFRESHED
REJECTED
RELAXED
RELIEVED
REMORSEFUL
RESTLESS
REVERENT
REWARDED
RIGHTEOUS

S

SAD
SATED
SATISFIED
SCARED
SENTIMENTAL
SERVILE
SETTLED
SEXY
SHOCKED
SILLY
SINISTER
SKEPTICAL
SMART
SNEAKY
SOLEMN
SORROWFUL
SPITEFUL
STARTLED
STINGY
STRANGE
STUFFED
STUPID
STUNNED
SUFFERING
SURE
SYMPATHETIC

T

TALKATIVE
TEMPTED
TENACIOUS
TENDER
TENSE
TENTATIVE
TERRIBLE
THREATENED
TICKLED
TIRED
THWARTED
TITILLATED
TRAPPED
TROUBLED
TRUSTING

U

UGLY
UNEASY
UNSETTLED

V

VIOLENT
VEHEMENT
VITAL
VULNERABLE
VIVACIOUS

W

WICKED
WONDERFUL
WEEPY
WORRIED

X

XENOPHOBIC

Y

YEARNING

Z

ZANY
ZESTFUL
ZINGY

The dilemma for you is between the risk of rejection or humiliation if you express your feelings and never getting what you want if you do not. The paradox is that unless we can feel and express sadness and pain we cannot feel and express happiness and joy.

If you express anger and rage, you will get back anger and fear. If you express sadness and hurt, you may get back support and understanding.

Use the list, *The Alphabet of Feelings,* as an exercise. Circle the feelings you have experienced.

Which feelings have you expressed to others? _____
_____

Which feelings are important to you? _____
_____

Can you add any feelings to the list?_____
_____

Hot Potato

Fights, especially those that end in abuse and violence, are about intolerable feelings. People in troubled relationships attempt to force the other person to change rather than experience a particularly uncomfortable feeling. For instance, a jealous person will try to restrict his partner's activity so he does not have to face his fear of loss or abandonment.

Ending the process of escalating conflict requires that one or both partners experience feelings that they have been unwilling to acknowledge in the past. Accepting your feelings as yours and recognizing that your mate does not have to change so that you do not have the feelings is a difficult step. This exercise will help you begin the process of taking responsibility for your feelings. The true test will occur when a situation occurs and you are experiencing feelings.

List the feelings you do not like.

1. _____   6. _____
2. _____   7. _____
3. _____   8. _____
4. _____   9. _____
5. _____   10. _____

List what you do about the feelings you do not like.
1. _____
2. _____
3. _____
4. _____
5. _____

How have you pressured your partner to alter her or his behavior so you don't have to experience these feelings?

_____

_____

_____

How I Look at the Violent Incident Now

For the past months, you have been gaining insight into your feelings, thoughts and behaviors. It is time to do an exercise similar to one you completed when you first entered the program. Complete this exercise, then compare it to the exercise on page 21, How I Looked at the *Violent Incident When it Occurred.*

THE EVENT

↓

MY FEELINGS AND THOUGHTS

↓

MY BEHAVIOR

What were my feeling just prior to the violence? _____

_____

_____

What are my feelings now? _____

_____

_____

What were my thoughts just prior to the violence? _____

_____

_____

What are my thoughts now? _____

_____

What was I trying to accomplish by being violent? _____

_____

_____

How do I explain the violence to others now? _____

_____

How do I still minimize or justify the violence? _____

_____

Social Isolation

The abusive man wants to insulate himself from the influences and demands of society and finds it safer to isolate himself and his family. Isolation protects him from experiencing challenges to his belief system, rejection, humiliation or domination. He erroneously views the world as menacing, undependable and likely to take advantage of or hurt him because he believes that he is weak and vulnerable.

Do you view other people as sources of help and support or do you see people as untrustworthy and dangerous? Examine the diagram on the next page and consider how many people in each category you know. "C" people are the men and women you know at work, participate with in sports and socialize with. You share small talk but there is little emotional investment. "B" people are the men and women that are your friends. You trust and share important thoughts and feelings with these people. "A" people are those men and women whom you have an intimate relationship with, including your mate.

On a piece of paper write the names of all "C" people you know. How many "C" people do you have in your life?_____
People who are isolated may know only a few "C" people. People who are not isolated and are active socially can easily know dozens of "C" people.

On a piece of paper write the names of all the "B" people you know. How many "B" people do you have in your life?_____
Isolated people may have one "B" person in their life but more commonly there is no "B" person. People who are not isolated generally have several "B" people in their lives.

How many "A" people do you have in you life?_____
Experience has shown it is common for the abusive and violent man to have only a few "C" type people in his life, maybe one but more often no "B" type people, and one "A" person—his mate.

Change is the Third Path
M. Lindsey, R. McBride and C. Platt

Relationship Pyramid—The People in Your Life

A = Significant others
B = Friends (companions, trusted confidants)
C = Associates (fellow workers, social circle, community)

**Batterer—
Isolated Man**

Emotional support and companionship invested in one person.

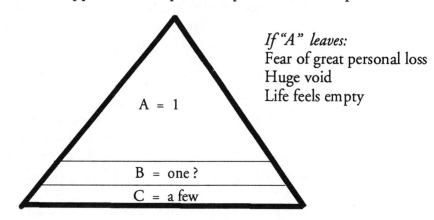

If "A" leaves:
Fear of great personal loss
Huge void
Life feels empty

A = 1

B = one ?

C = a few

**Assertive—
Socially Active
Man**

Finds emotional support and companionship in self and many others.

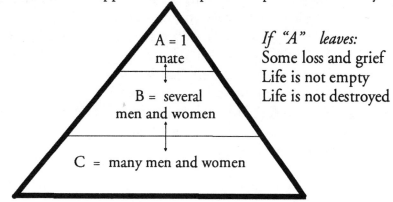

If "A" leaves:
Some loss and grief
Life is not empty
Life is not destroyed

A = 1
mate

B = several
men and women

C = many men and women

Where do you get emotional support and companionship?
From the lists you made draw the triangle as it applies to your A,B,C people.

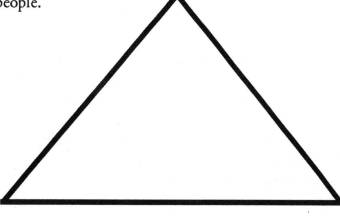

Change is the Third Path
M. Lindsey, R. McBride and C. Platt

This type of lifestyle creates a paradox.
Isolation may protect you temporarily from a world you see as unreliable, untrustworthy and threatening. Conversely, it eliminates the possibility of you receiving the benefits and rewards a network of people provides—information, camaraderie and support.

The problems that arise from being isolated are greater in the long-run than the uncertainty or discomfort the abusive and violent man is trying to avoid. He may frequently claim he doesn't want or need anyone else's help and rejects available information and resources. Instead of asking for help because he fears being vulnerable, looking stupid, being obligated and so on, he produces additional chaos in his life. Not having a network to turn to for information or help, the abusive and violent man does one of two things. He may struggle unnecessarily with problems until frustrated and overwhelmed, wastes his time and energy, and becomes angry and enraged. The other method is to not respond or to try to avoid problems. In the short-run this may work. However, the number and size of the problems will continue to grow until they overwhelm him.

The abusive and violent man wants closeness and support and is commonly very needy. However feeling vulnerable and untrusting of people, he avoids sharing his life. He finds an intimate relationship and seeks to obtain all his needs from this person. No matter how hard she may try, this is an impossible task. When she fails to meet all his needs, he blames his mate for not trying hard enough or doing it wrong. He often frustrates himself trying to get something she cannot give. He may move on to another relationship still seeking the impossible or she may leave the relationship. If she leaves before he establishes another relationship, the abusive and violent man commonly feels empty, annihilated and lost. He frequently describes this huge void as having most of his life ripped away or destroyed.

Have you invested all your needs for closeness and support in one significant person?

☐ Yes   ☐ No

If so, think about how you view the control this person has over you. Is this an impossible responsibility for this person?

☐ Yes   ☐ No

Write about why are you isolated. _____
_____
_____

_____

Write about what you can do to make changes and get out of your isolation. _____
_____
_____

Building and Maintaining a Facade

Nearly all people try to conceal or minimize actual or perceived failure or personal deficits from time to time, but they do not feel the need to hide their real personality from the others on a continuous basis. As an abusive and violent man you must pretend to be something you are not. You have learned to conceal your true self, your real agenda, your feelings and your needs. You have come to understand that letting others know who you really are can only lead to failure or punishment. You maintain a facade not only for the world but for yourself so you can avoid facing who you really are inside.

The process of constructing a facade is complicated and started when you were young and began to reject feedback from your parents or extended family. You probably received mixed messages and can remember saying or deciding that you were not going to "take this shit anymore" or that "nobody will tell me what to do ever again."

You began to develop and act roles to reduce your punishment, gain acceptance and get by. Having made this decision, you began to separate the real you from the person the world saw and continued to fall further behind in your ability to make your life work. In effect, you have replaced your feelings with roles you think the world will find acceptable. For your survival, you believe you must not allow anyone, not even yourself, to discover your weaknesses.

Your facade protects you from consequences by providing a convincing front with which the world can interact. You may ordinarily appear relaxed, sensible, prosperous and peaceful. Even though you may appear truthful and maybe even healthy, you are not. In public you cleverly play roles so only your best side shows. People often see you as interesting and wish to be with you, yet you dare not let people in because in reality, you are a very fragile person.

You do not feel safe being close. You fear you really have nothing to offer people and that they will be disappointed and leave you. You are driven by emotional pain and needs you neither understand nor take the time to examine. You neither think about your motives nor the consequences of your actions.

Your facade hides a great deal of fear, shame, guilt, rage and sexualized thoughts or activities. Your facade hides the real self that harbors your goals and wishes of which society is unaware. These wishes might range from the desire to rape and murder women to being attracted to prostitutes. You may fantasize about sex with other men or about being able to seduce any woman.

YOU BUILT THE WALL FOR PROTECTION

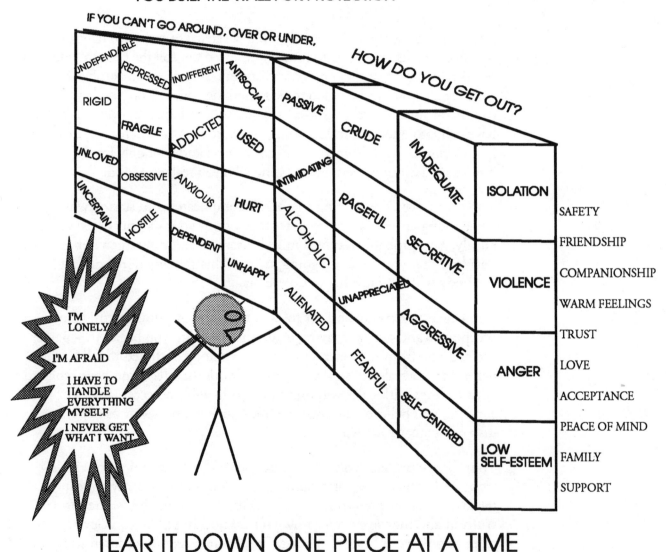

TEAR IT DOWN ONE PIECE AT A TIME

These fantasies are tools that help you avoid facing the lie of your false self. Reflected in the fantasies is the real person, a man who is and has been

Change is the Third Path
M. Lindsey, R. McBride and C. Platt

alienated from society, friends, and family—an inadequate and angry man who feels that no matter how hard he tries, he will never succeed.

For example, one man told how he was attacked by his wife. She threw things, hit and scratched him; he had the marks to prove it. He failed to mention that he had carried her into the bedroom and held her hostage for three hours until she attacked.

Another batterer told a story about throwing a heavy glass against the wall. It bounced off the wall and hit his mate in the head, cutting her. In actuality, he had fractured her skull with a plaster object and she almost died. These stories are distortions of reality that make the men who tell them look better. Denial and minimization of your violence are a necessary part of your front.

It's likely that you want some success at the goals you have set for yourself. These goals may include loving and caring for a mate and family; being a capable and successful worker; living up to masculine values about protecting family and country; enjoying life and being happy.

Your life may be something quite different. You probably resist any feedback that does not match your internal world, goals or agenda. You have begun to suffer the consequences of your inability to get along with people. Without help your problems will get worse.

If you continue to find reasons to blame others for your behavior, you will miss the best part of life. Society will become increasingly punishing as you keep getting into trouble with the authorities. You will fail to advance; friends will abandon you; your mate has fled or will flee because you remain unavailable emotionally and often physically.

As a young man, you may be able to start over, to hide the failures and losses. As you get older, your ability to hide from the truth diminishes and your ability to recover emotionally from the loss of self-worth becomes increasingly difficult. Your end may be suicide, early death from alcohol, drugs, ill health or a pointless existence.

You may have a lot to offer but it is buried so deep that even you do not see your potential. You may feel and care more than many of the people around you, yet you will not expose your vulnerable side to the world because of fear. The loving and caring part of who you are gets pushed aside by your unpredictability, violence and unresponsiveness to others. The people around you will come to look upon you as indifferent, remote, self-absorbed, difficult, unavailable, and inflexible.

Before it's too late.
What kind of life do you want?

Assertiveness and Other Life Skills

You are assertive when you state what you feel, think and want honestly and completely.

Being assertive is directly asking for what you want or need.

It also means directly refusing what you don't want.

Passive people tend to consider only the rights of others while aggressive people tend to consider only their rights.

Men who batter have trouble being assertive. This lack of assertiveness arises from two separate sources:

A feeling of entitlement, that is, the belief that their way or needs take precedence over all others'.

The feeling that their needs are not important.

As children we are innately assertive and act as we are, without pretense. These spontaneous actions elicit a variety of consequences. They can be rewarded, ignored or punished. If our way of getting childhood needs met is not successful, we grow to adulthood without the important ability to ask constructively for what we want.

The man who enters treatment for violence often has a very difficult time asking for what he wants. He fears rejection or disappointment. He attempts to get his needs met by hints and inferences, by over-giving, or by assuming that somehow his mate will "know what I need." Or he may decide that he will take what he needs despite the consequences to his mate or children.

As an abusive and violent man, you may avoid conflict because it frightens you and because you lack skills in dealing with yourself and others. As you go about life you experience stress in the form of day-to-day problems

Change is the Third Path
M. Lindsey, R. McBride and C. Platt

which you do not confront. Tension continually builds in you. You may feel weak or worthless because you are not solving the problems in your life. You probably feel you have no control. Typically, you keep stuffing feelings, letting bad feelings build until you explode. These may be mini-explosions such as yelling, honking your car horn, "flipping off" other drivers, or cursing at traffic delays. However, these little bursts of anger don't make you feel better for long and you learn nothing. They may increase the likelihood of a greater explosion because they often pass without any consequences. They may eventually lead to an explosion during a conflict with your partner.

As an abusive and violent man, you vacillate between the extremes of being passive and aggressive.

The examples below are repeated to demonstrate a lack of assertiveness.

> One man convinced himself that he could create a sanctuary where his wife could grow and heal from the pain of her life. She flirted with men, used drugs, and almost bankrupted him with her spending sprees. However, he was unable to say no to her because he was afraid she would leave him. He was too frightened to tell her he could not live like this. His illusion was, "If I take care of her, she will change and then I can get what I need."

> A second man was so afraid his wife would be seduced by another man that he did not allow her to leave the house without him. He made sure all the doors and windows were sealed with tape when he left the house. He checked the tape on his return to see if the seals were broken. That way he would know if she went out or let someone in the house.

Neither over-giving nor controlling provided relief from these men's fears, and both became violent toward their wives. Some abusive men are passive men who cannot say no while others are so threatened and insecure that they say no all of the time in an attempt to control everything.

Men who are reasonably assertive about what they want or need and secure about who they are and how they feel do not batter their partners.

Three important parts to being assertive:
✔ What we say; the words we use.

✔ How we say it; the tone of voice we use; the speed at which we say it.

✔ Body position when we say it; do we look assertive; are we facing the person; do we maintain eye contact while talking?

Limit Setting

All people have limits regarding their ability to manage emotionally charged situations. Individuals who become violent often fail to understand the idea of limit setting. In order to set limits, either they try to control the other person or they try to take on more than is possible.

In the first case above, the man's wife was spending large amounts of money and using drugs, he needed to accept two facts. First, he could not emotionally tolerate the situation. Second, his wife would not change. He then could say, "I cannot live this way and I am going to get a divorce."

In the second case above, the man needed to recognize that he was the problem not his wife. Attempts to set limits on another person in order to calm our fears will not work and can be abusive.

Legitimate limit setting occurs when we are able to say, "I cannot accept. . . and I am willing to take the consequences." In the first case, the man was able to finally say I am not willing to live this way. His wife left and continued to use drugs.

Limit setting is not to be used as an attempt to manipulate or coerce another person. It is to be used when we have reached a point where a true limit exists.

Four Behaviors for Dealing With People—Your Choice

WHEN YOU ARE	PASSIVE	PASSIVE-AGGRESSIVE	AGGRESSIVE	ASSERTIVE
You are:	Emotionally dishonest Indirect, inhibited, reactive Self-denying (silent martyr) Blaming, apologetic	Emotionally dishonest Indirect, self-denying at first Self-enhancing at expense of others later on	Inappropriately honest Direct, expressive, attacking, Blaming, controlling, self-enhancing at expense of others	Appropriately honest Direct, self-enhancing, Expressive, self-confident
Your feelings are:	I'm not okay; you're not okay. I'm not okay; you're okay. Hurt, anxious Victimized Possibly angry later	Insecure, fearful, then angry and vengeful	I'm okay; you're not okay. I'm not okay; you're not okay. Righteous, superior Deprecatory at the time and possibly guilty later	Respectful of self and others at the time and later
Beliefs about yourself:	I have to be perfect or I'm worthless. I don't count. Others are more important than I.	I can't trust anyone. I can outsmart others to get my needs met.	I am entitled. I must have control. I have to look out for myself. The world revolves around me.	I am happy because I can meet my own goals while respecting the needs of others.

An example of different responses to the provocative statement, "Your ideas are stupid and immature."

"Uh...I guess you're right...I don't know too much..."	You say nothing but then stand the person up for a date, later saying you "just forgot."	"Go to Hell! We all know your I.Q. is below normal because your mother was a dirty *#."	"I don't feel you know me well enough to make that judgment. Right or wrong, I have a right to my opinion."

Problem Solving—Conflict Resolution Strategy

Problem solving is a complex process that cannot be covered adequately in this workbook. However, the following problem solving steps can help you achieve increased solution oriented interactions with others.

Step 1: *Slow down.*
> Observe: thoughts and feelings
> Listen to what is being said.

Step 2: *Define the problem.*
> Internal: my thoughts and feelings
> External: others behaviors

Step 3: *State the desired outcome*
> Is this outcome a real possibility?
> What will prevent me from achieving this outcome?
> Is the goal of this outcome constructive?

Step 4: *Gather the information necessary to solve the problem.*
> Do I have all the information or facts I need?
> If not, where can I get the information?
> Or, from whom can I get the information?

Step 5: *List the alternative outcomes.*
> What is the best choice?
> Is the correct choice hard for me to do?
> Why it is hard for me to do?
> What can I do—not what I want to do or should do?
> If it is the correct choice, how can I do it?

Step 6: *Consider the consequences of the outcome.*
> Consequences to myself
> Consequences to others

Step 7: *Implement the response or solution to the problem.*

Slowing down is a crucial part of problem solving. Always slow down before responding to a problem. Use a Time Out when interactions are intense. Do not react. Do not let your emotions drive your actions. Feelings act as an alarm to tell us when something is wrong but they do not tell us what is wrong or what to do about it.

Take the time to think about what actually is the problem. Is it what it appears to be or something else? Do not jump to conclusions. Instead of blaming someone else or something, examine the problem by thinking

Change is the Third Path
M. Lindsey, R. McBride and C. Platt

about the following:

> What is my part in the problem?
> What do I feel, other than anger?
> Do I have all the facts?
> What is a possible solution?

People do not always correctly identify the problem and nobody has all the answers to a problem. You need to seek out as much information as you can and determine the facts of the situation. By seeking input from others, you will be able to greatly improve the possibility that the problem has been identified correctly. You will also likely increase the number of possible solutions which will enhance the probability of finding a correct solution. It does no good to slow down, get information, establish what is wrong and devise a plan then have it fall apart when you try to take action to solve the problem. Prior to taking action, consider the following:

Do not try to predict how the other person will respond.
Be prepared for them to escalate, blame or disagree.
Be prepared for them to have different ideas about what the problem is.
Be prepared for them to have different solutions.

Let the other person respond and have their position. Listen.
Acknowledge your partner's feelings and position without minimizing or criticizing.

Be prepared to manage your feelings so you do not allow your feelings to stop the process.
Negotiate and compromise about what is likely to work.

Avoid using the following words: should, must, have to, gotta or can't.
These words create rigidity.
These are essentially rule words that establish how "things" will be and have an "or else" quality to them.

Use the words could and would, as in:
"I would like. . . ." or "This could be a solution."
These words leave room for the other person to respond.

Avoid the word "you." Use the word "I," as in:
"I would like. . . ." or "I could do. . . ."

Stay focused on the problem.
If necessary, write down the problem and do not wander off the task.
If your partner or the other person has a different issue, acknowledge it and set a time to talk about it later.
Agree to try the solution that has been negotiated.

Understanding the Role of Thoughts in Problem Solving

Dodge's model:

The social information model explains how people translate the thoughts generated by observations into actions. Dodge's theory is based on the fact that human beings are forever decoding the world they observe, searching for relevant data, i.e. information or cues. When we perceive a piece of information as relevant, we interpret it according to the structure of "rules" that already exists in our memories. This structure is derived from our experiences and the goals we have set. Our goals are what give life meaning and as such, may feel necessary to our survival.

Dodge points out that new data are always competing for recognition, and some we find useful enough to adopt. After we integrate new data with our existing rules and goals, we may choose to respond to the information. Our response is generated through a process in which we consider both the adequacy and the consequences of the action we propose. After deciding to act, we shape our decision by considering when, where and how we will perform the action. The final step in this process of encoding is action itself.

From Dodge's model it is clear that problem solving can go wrong at several points.

> We can fail to notice the problem because it is outside of our scanning area.
> We can observe the problem but fail to attend to it.
> We can notice the problem, attend to it and make an incorrect interpretation.
> We can detect the problem, attend to it, interpret it correctly but then have the wrong response.

We can improve our problem solving ability by understanding the role thoughts play in our lives. When we interpret events, we do so by using the complex set of thoughts, ideas, attitudes, beliefs and values we developed throughout our life. To the extent that our belief systems are based in reality and are rational or accurate, our interpretations will be fairly accurate. When our belief systems are irrational and not based in reality, we will make incorrect interpretations.

For example, a man believed his wife was having an affair and was going to leave him. He escalated and set their bed on fire. First, his response was violent and dangerous. He could have done something different. Second, his wife was not having an affair even though he believed she was.

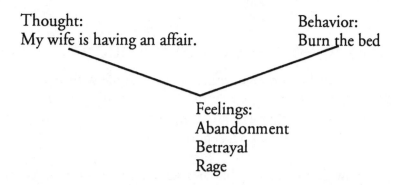

Thought:
My wife is having an affair.

Behavior:
Burn the bed

Feelings:
Abandonment
Betrayal
Rage

This man was abandoned as a child. When his father died, his mother placed him in an orphanage. He lived there for twelve years until his mother took him back. He developed a deep set of beliefs about attachment and abandonment. This system of beliefs controlled much of his behavior regarding relationships with women. Because he held deep beliefs that he would be abandoned again, he interpreted many normal behaviors of his wife as threats to the relationship. He lived in a state of hyper-vigilance. He was trying to avoid loss. The fact was that his fear was being generated from within him rather than from the behavior of his wife.

We all have developed deeply held beliefs about ourselves and the world. These systems of beliefs have been called "schemas." We can think of them as "schematics" that organize our internal world and direct behavior. Schemas based in trauma or abuse, especially in childhood, are emotionally charged and hard to change.

In short-term therapy a person who has a history of violence and abuse will not change their childhood schemas. The individual will learn skills such as anger management that will enable them to have greater behavioral control but the schemas will be left in place.

These schemas remain latent waiting to resurface during periods of stress or conflict. Short-term education based therapy can help. It will not provide complete recovery.

Problems in Communication

Inappropriate Versus Appropriate Non-verbal Messages

Non-verbal messages must be compatible with the verbal message. Saying "I hurt" in an angry manner transmits anger not hurt.
Non-verbal messages are transmitted by tone of voice, eye contact, posture, body language, and intimidation.

How do my non-verbal messages match what I am trying to say?

_____

Biases Concerning Past Information

Biases such as memories, hurt, stereotypes and unresolved conflicts interfere with both speaking and listening.

How do my biases interfere with my efforts to communicate?

_____

_____

Assumptions

Relying on internal perceptions rather than listening, trusting and checking out information distorts communication. For example: assuming you already know what the other person will think or say.

What assumptions do I make when listening or talking to others?

_____

_____

Selective Listening or Talking

You may unconsciously filter out what you do not want to say or hear yet think you have got the whole picture.
How do I do filter out what I don't want to hear or say?

_____

_____

Deception and Digression

Deception is withholding information, being vague, telling half-truths, lying.

Digression is rambling: exaggerating or going on and on with detail and not getting to the point you are trying to make.

How do I digress? How do I deceive in my conversation?

_____

_____

Use "I" statements about feelings, such as "I feel sad" not "you" statements, such as "You made me sad."

Be precise with "because," as in "I feel hurt _because_ you yelled at me" instead of using general accusations such as "I am angry because you are a bitch."

Relationships

A common struggle in relationships revolves around how much of ourselves we will "lose" in the relationship. During courtship we tend to focus heavily on the relationship and our friendships and activities fall by the wayside. Eventually life returns to normal and an adjustment is made to balance the relationship with other demands. Relationships that become violent often involve intense battles over closeness and separation.

Another common problem for people involved in long-term relationships is finding out that their partner does not meet their needs or expectations. Men in treatment often express thoughts like: "My partner does not understand. . . ," "I do not understand why my mate does. . . ." "I do not know what my partner wants, she is never satisfied."

These problems arise because people trying to establish a relationship often go about starting a relationship for the wrong reasons and in the wrong way. An example of the wrong reasons can be shown from experiences with groups of men in treatment. We have asked men in treatment to list on a chalkboard the qualities they would look for in a woman when trying to establish a relationship. When finished, the list invariably contained only physical or material items—does she have big breasts, a nice butt, great legs, a great body, beautiful features, a job, a car, money, great looking clothes, children; is she a good cook or housekeeper; will she take good care of me; can I get sex from her or is she good in bed.

The same men were offered alternative considerations, such as. Can we have a discussion? Do we have compatible ideas on morals, politics, children and so on? Do we agree about how a relationship could work? Are our life goals congruous? Can we disagree and work on differences or problems respectfully? Do we like each other and are we friends? At first in every instance, most of the men laughed and thought these ideas were silly. It was difficult for these men to understand until they took the time to think about why their previous relationships had not worked. Most people have some response to physical attraction however, it has little to do with building a satisfying long-term relationship.

Using the Relationship Pyramid on page 99, we can examine how many people go about starting a long-term or permanent relationship in the wrong way. As we explained earlier, in your relationship network "C" people are the men and women you know at work, participate with in sports and socialize with. You share small talk but there is little emotional investment. "B" people are the men and women that are your friends. You trust and share important thoughts and feelings with these people. "A" people are the couple of men and women whom you have an intimate relationship with, including your mate. For our current discussion, we need an additional level. A "D" person is a person not involved in your relationship network or a complete stranger.

Socially active people usually have a substantial network made up of "A," "B," and "C" people. Sometimes, "C" people leave your relationship pyramid or move up to be "B" people. "B" people can leave your relationship network or move down to be "C" people or perhaps they could move up to be an "A" person. If for whatever reason, you have no "A" person or an "A" person leaves your life, where do you find another "A" person if you want to?

Often, people who are socially isolated have no or a limited relationship network. The mistake that many people make when looking for an "A" person relationship is going out of their relationship network to find a "D" person to make into an "A" person. Often the result of trying to put a "D" person immediately into an "A" person position is summed up in all the complaints listed above about not knowing or liking the person with whom they are deeply involved.

The inference is, it is probably better to have a "B" person become an "A" person than a "D" person. This does not eliminate "D" people from entering your life. It means they need to enter at the "C" level and after getting know them, they possibly could move up to a "B" position or out of your life.

While this process may seem a bit mechanical, time consuming and involved, it is a tool for you to look at how you develop your relationships. You have many choices to make about your relationships. It is the decisions you make that help determine the success of your relationships. Presumably you do not want to end up in a chaotic relationship filled with resentment and disappointment. The answer to having a satisfying long-term relationship is in taking the time to find out who you are involved with and develop the relationship.

As you study the diagrams on the next page, think of all the things you want from your relationship. Once these desires are identified you can make an effort to solve the problems that keep you from having more of whatever it is you want.

List the things you want in a long-term relationship:

_____

_____

_____

_____

_____

Change is the Third Path
M. Lindsey, R. McBride and C. Platt

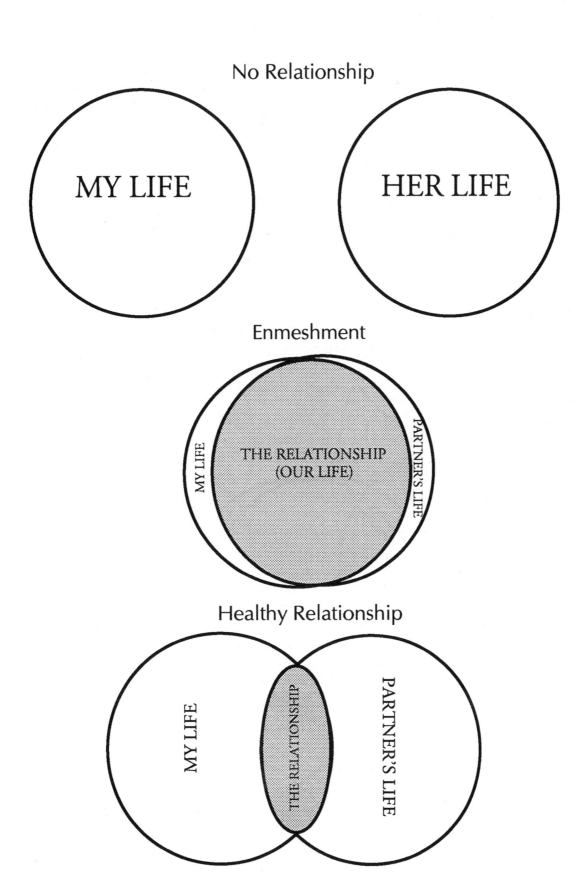

No Relationship

MY LIFE

HER LIFE

Enmeshment

MY LIFE

THE RELATIONSHIP
(OUR LIFE)

PARTNER'S LIFE

Healthy Relationship

MY LIFE

THE RELATIONSHIP

PARTNER'S LIFE

Skills of Self-talk

Developing a new violence-free lifestyle includes developing new rituals. Relaxation, affirmation and creative visualization are techniques you can use to slow down and gain control of your thoughts, feelings and behaviors. You can use these skills when you are building tension, during a Time Out or to aid you in daily living.

Relaxation

When you begin to feel tense and stressed and you are building toward an explosion, one way to relieve the tension is to relax. In a tense and stressful situation, your breathing becomes quick and shallow and your heart rate increases, preparing your body for fight or flight.

There are many ways to achieve a state of relaxation. One excellent method is a deep breathing exercise. Forcing yourself to breathe slowly and deeply calms the body. The body and mind work in concert with each other. When the body relaxes, the mind follows and vice versa. Concentrating on your breathing takes your mind off the obsessive thoughts that you are using to create and maintain anxiety.

✓ Slowly breathe in while expanding your abdomen and lifting your shoulders on a count of four.
✓ Hold your breathe for a count of four.
✓ Exhale slowly while relaxing your abdomen and slowly bring down your shoulders on a count of eight.
✓ Hold for a count of four.
✓ Repeat this four times.

Affirmations

Negative beliefs rule much of our lives.
We perpetuate these negative beliefs in our views of the world and our actions. An affirmation is a strong, positive statement saying that something we want is already so. It can be general or specific. By using affirmations, we can begin to counter our negative belief systems which so often pull us down, blocking our full potential. This is a powerful technique but requires effort. It is not easy to change old negative habits. The power in the technique lies in the fact that it can change our attitudes and expectations about life, thereby changing our sense of what is possible.

✓ Always phrase affirmations in the present tense (as if they are already occurring), not in the future. Example: "I (your name) now have a wonderful new job."
✓ Always phrase affirmations in the most positive way—Affirm what you want, not what you don't want. Negative example: "I no longer will oversleep in the morning." Positive example, "I will wake at 6 A.M. feeling rested."

Change is the Third Path
M. Lindsey, R. McBride and C. Platt

✓ In general, the shorter and simpler the affirmation the more effective it will be.

✓ The affirmation you choose should be expressed in your own words.

✓ Always remember when you are doing affirmations that you are creating something new. You are not trying to redo or change what already exists.

✓ Affirmations are not meant to contradict or change your feelings or emotions. If you are sad over a loss, you cannot affirm that you are happy about the loss.

✓ Try as much as possible to create a feeling of belief that an experience can be true.

✓ Put your full mental and emotional energy into the affirmation.

✓ Affirmations cannot change other people's behaviors—changes can only occur from within you, which may in turn have an indirect effect on your interactions with others and their interaction with you.

✓ When using affirmations, use your name to personalize the positive self-statement.

✓ If you find it difficult to maintain a positive self-statement, it's probably because you are contradicting your statement with negative thoughts. This is an indication that you need to move to a clearing process (removing negative thoughts about yourself).

Affirmations can create a new point of view about your life situation which will enable you to have more satisfying experiences.

Creative Visualization

Creative visualization is the technique of using your imagination to create what you want in life. Imagination is a powerful source. It gives all human beings the power to create. In creative visualization you are using your imagination to create a clear image of something you wish to manifest. Creative visualization can be used effectively with affirmations. Remember that creative visualization takes practice.

Creative Visualization Exercise

✓ Think of something you would like (something you can easily imagine attaining).

✓ Relax your body completely. Clear your mind of all your worries. Count down slowly from ten to one, feeling yourself relaxing more as you approach the number one.

✓ Begin to imagine yourself having or doing the thing that you want for yourself.

✓ Make some positive affirmative statements to yourself while visualizing. The more vivid the visualization, the more effective the visualization.

✓ Use all your senses when you visualize (sight, smell, hearing, touch, taste). The better you are at capturing the visualization with your senses, the better the results.

✓ If negative thoughts or images distort your visualization, attempt to refocus on your original visualization.

The Tunnel

This concept is important if you are going to continue with the process of change. Many years of intervention with over 10,000 violent men has taught us a hard truth. Violent people will continue to live in chaos, die, or change. Change is painful and frightening. The process of recovery requires a type of psychic death of the old self so you make way for the new person. There will come a time when the process is half done but the end of it cannot be seen. You will find returning to the old way of functioning unacceptable. This point is dangerous for all concerned. If you continue your journey, you will find satisfaction with your life.

Life of chaos

Economic, legal, sexual, and
relationship problems
Stress   Anger
Rage   Violence
Fear   Depression
Guilt   Lies
Denial   Facade
Isolation   Manipulation
Emptiness   Distorted self-worth
Passivity and aggression
Need for control

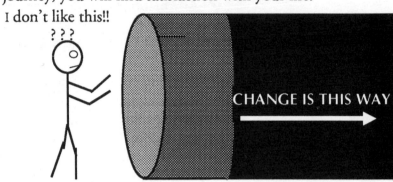

I don't like this!!
???

CHANGE IS THIS WAY →

Unknown Journey
Unknown Time
Unknown Destination

I can't see either end!
I'm so tired of this crap!

PAIN

SUICIDE

← RETURN TO LIFE OF CHAOS

LIFE OF SATISFACTION THIS WAY →

Life of satisfaction

Managing stress
Aware of feelings
Bright and hopeful
Assertive
Self-confident
Socially involved
Aware of limits
Fulfilled

YOU HAVE BEGUN A DIFFICULT JOURNEY TO A NEW AND MORE SATISFYING LIFE. IF YOU WANT TO CONTINUE IT'S UP TO YOU.

Your Children

The notion that parents are entitled to respect simply because they are parents is preposterous. The stream of obligation runs strongly the other way.
   John Macy

Men in treatment for abusive and violent behavior and separated from their mates often are concerned about losing contact with their children. The reason for their concern commonly arises from a situation over which they feel they have little or no control.

His mate has left and is in hiding with the children.
His mate has a restraining or no contact order in place against him.
The court has forbidden him visitation or restricted visitations to a controlled environment with supervision by a third party.
He realizes that his children see him as abusive and violent and want little or nothing to do with him.

The abusive and violent man usually expresses the thought that the situation is unfair and he has a right to be with his children. He frequently claims his mate has lied and is using the children to manipulate him, the police exaggerated the incident, the court only cares about the rights' of women or social services personnel are feminist trying to destroy the family. The fact is the domestic violence perpetrator often minimizes and denies his behavior to himself and others. It is difficult for the abusive and violent man to accept that his mate and children are afraid of him or that the criminal justice system sees his behavior as a threat to society.

He fears without being able to exert some control over the situation:

His ex-mate will turn their children against him.
He will lose input on raising the children.
Another man will raise "his" children.
The children will forget him.

He fears that the loss of his children is beyond his control. This does not have to be true for you. If you want a relationship with your children, you can have it. It may take some time and it will take a lot of work but you can do it.

Developing a relationship with your children will not just happen. You must have a commitment to parenthood. You need to put thought and effort into creating a healthy environment for the relationship to grow. Think of parenting of as a group of skills. They do not always come naturally but you can learn these skills and become a good parent.

Start working on the relationship with your children by clearly understanding what you are doing and why. Organize your process by knowing what you need to do and how you are going to do it. Get help with ideas and evaluating your process from specialized counselors, reading parenting materials and taking classes. Does it look like work? It is. Like everything else you have learned to do, it will get easier with practice. If you are working on this process for the right reason, you and your children will reap benefits far greater than your efforts.

Understanding what you are doing means defining the result you want. Think and state carefully what you want to do. Statements such as, "I want to get my kids back within six months" or "I have a right to see my kids," do not mean much. These kinds of statements sound as though you think of your children as objects that you want to possess. Also keep an open mind about how relationships can work. The relationship with your children may need to be different from what it was or what you thought a parent-child relationship should be. A short, one or two sentence, statement defining the kind of relationship that would be beneficial to your children and you could help you focus on what you want to accomplish.

Why you want to have a relationship with your children is significant. Do you want to:

> Get even with your ex-mate by fighting for custody of the children?
> Make sure your ex-mate does not get it all her way?
> Minimizes or avoid child support?
> Avoid more pain from feelings of loss and abandonment?
> Prove you are okay and a good person?
> Share in the responsibility of raising your children?
> Have some input on raising your children?
> Develop a supportive and loving environment for your children?

Part of the process is knowing what to do and in what order to develop a healthy caring relationship. You may have to start slow building on one small accomplishment after another. That could mean working on your issues first so your children can view you as safe, dependable, reasonable and supportive. They are looking to you as a role model on how to live.

The following are things you may need to do in your process of developing a relationship with your children.

End your drug or alcohol addiction. As a chemically addicted person you cannot have a caring relationship. You have only one relationship and that is with your drug of choice.

Continue working on your issues of truthfulness, power, control, anger, abuse and violence in a domestic violence therapy group.

Tactfully request supervised visitation with your children. As you demonstrate your reasonableness, request extended visitations. Men that have restraining or no contact orders in place by the courts need to start slow.

Improve your parenting skills so you feel more secure in raising your children. Frequently people have children but have little information on how best to raise them.

Consider carefully the time and energy needed for shared custody. Sometimes fathers who have shared custody of or visitations with their children find they have not allowed the time and energy needed for the children.

Decide how you are going to provide safety, dependability, predictability and support for your children. Children need to feel their world is all these things and they need to have structure, respect and love.

Getting your life together is a priority. Without a rational lifestyle, you will have little hope in developing a healthy relationship with your children. Children do not grow-up well or form healthy relationships in a chaotic environment.

Commonly, a father in your situation worries that the child's mother will tell lies about him, say bad things about him or undermine his position as a parent. The reality of this may or may not be true. You cannot control what another person says or does. Give your children credit for knowing how they feel about you. If your children see you as consistently safe, dependable, predictable and loving, they will know the truth. They will respond to you as they perceive you without consideration for what others may. Developing the relationship with your children depends on how you control your thoughts, feelings and behaviors.

Parenting is not an easy task. However, many men have worked hard and succeeded in developing a caring relationship with their children. The following stories are about men who at one time were in situations similar yours.

Ray

Ray, father of a six-month old boy, was attending a domestic violence group when his divorce was final. The court denied him visitations with the child at the request of the mother because of his previously abusive and violent behavior. He began petitioning the court for visitation with his child. After several months, the court granted supervised visitations for three hours each month. When the child was two years old, the court granted visitation with the child every other weekend along with a vacation and holiday schedule.

The mother quickly quit her job and took a job eighty miles away. She thwarted every effort he made to see the child. He took her to court. She denied his allegations and everything continued as before. Ray was frustrated and angry about the situation and brought it up for discussion in his therapy group. The group suggested Ray keep a detailed journal of every activity and conversation with his ex-wife concerning visitations with his son. At the next court appearance things were different. Ray made a copy of the journal for the judge. After the judge admonished Ray's ex-wife, Ray had no more problems obtaining visitations.

Ray's ex-wife remained angry and continued to insult and verbally abuse him each time he picked up and returned their child. This process upset their child to the point where each time Ray approached his ex-wife's home the child began to cry. He tried to discuss the matter with the child's mother but to no avail. As the child grew older, Ray developed a strategy with the child to avoid the conflict. When Ray picked up his son, he would meet him on the front lawn of the home. When he returned his son, he would walk his son part way to the door then watch until he was inside. As the years past, Ray got what he wanted, a warm and loving relationship with his son.

Ray's commitment was to be a good father, have a loving relationship with his son, and not fight with his ex-wife. At first, his ex-wife attempted to block his efforts. However, he persisted in reasonable ways to minimize conflict and to develop the relationship.

Matthew

Matthew fled the state after battering his wife. He left behind three children he had fathered by two women. Two years after he had begun a new relationship, the police arrested him on domestic violence charges in Colorado. Unaware of his earlier history of drug use and violence, the district court sent him to a domestic violence therapy group. His current relationship ended and he decided against beginning a new relationship until he had resolved some of his issues.

Change is the Third Path
M. Lindsey, R. McBride and C. Platt

A year after entering treatment Matthew realized that in order to have a better life in the future he needed to straighten out the chaos from his past that was hanging over him. When he returned to his home state to visit and make amends, he discovered that he had lost all rights to his children. Because of his past drug use and violent behavior, he was considered dangerous. Welfare and the courts were after him for not supporting his children. He learned his oldest child, a son, was living with the child's mother and her boyfriend—both addicted to alcohol and heroine and living on welfare.

Matthew returned to his new state overwhelmed by the chaos he had left behind and determined to build relationships with his children. With help, he put together a plan that he hoped would correct the mess. He began reimbursing the welfare department, paying child support, paying off old fines, petitioning the courts for hearings to resolve outstanding issues and writing letters to social services about his concerns over his son's welfare. It took Matthew several years to clean up the mess he had help create. In the process, he regained parental status for all of his children and visitation rights including vacations. Eventually, the court gave him custody of his son and he brought him to Colorado to live with him.

Matthew came to realize that the chaos he had created would eventually bury him and that he needed to take control of his life. Then he saw that his behavior had directly affected the lives of his children. For Matthew part of learning to live a new way meant cleaning up his past. He knew the damage was too large to fix at once so he made a plan and slowly, one step at a time, made progress. He made a commitment and learned to be a parent. Although he had abandoned the children for several years, he felt good knowing that, as they approach adolescence, he now influences his children's lives in positive ways.

Richard

While in the process of recovery from abusive and violent behavior, Richard and his wife tried unsuccessfully to make their marriage work. Although both parties were angry, they worked out a polite and equitable divorce. Their two teenage children live with their mother. They became distant to both parents and seemed interested only in the material things their parents could provide.

After three years of minimal contact, Richard thought he had lost the relationship with his children and did not know how to repair it. In his mind, he still pictured his children as they were when he left. However, they were now young adults. In therapy, Richard got ideas about what the problem might be and what he could do to work on it. He arranged a casual outing with each of the teenage children during which he brought up his concerns about their relationship and his desire to improve it. He admitted that no matter the excuses, for the past few years, he had been a lousy father. He had not made enough effort to be available when they needed him and understood why they thought of him only as a provider of material things. He told each child that he wanted an emotional relationship with them.

Three months later one of the children called with a personal problem and asked for his assistance. While listening carefully and gently asking question, he made suggestions until the teen came up with a solution they found satisfactory. During the months that followed, both children began calling to discuss things with him and they began to spend more time together as a family. As young adults, both of the children had difficulty starting with their lives. Each young adult came to live with him for a period of time while they worked out what they needed to do. He offered them structure and was supportive of their efforts. The children became strong, self reliant adults and Richard has the warm caring relationship he wanted with them.

Richard recognized that just being a father was not enough. If he wanted to be a parent and have a caring relationship with his children, he had to involve himself in their lives. He understood that his children had made the transition from childhood to young adults without his input. It would be difficult re-entering their lives until he earned their trust and respect. Richard offered his support and love. Slowly they learned to be a family again.

For many abusive and violent men in chaotic relationships, much of the conflict with their mate is around their children. This kind of process is emotionally, psychologically and physically destructive to the children and makes it more difficult for the parents to maintain healthy caring relationships with their children. Don't take the "bait." Focus on the specific problem in the present—not what injuries occurred in the past. Children usually have no control over the parental decisions imposed on them. As a parent, you are responsible for your children's emotional and physical well-being and can make choices that help or hinder their development. See the break-up through their eyes. Always remember, if you want to enjoy a relationship with your children, it is your responsibility, not theirs, to lead the way and find ways to make it work. There are no quick fixes in repairing and developing relationships. It requires that you be consistent and reliable over time. You are the parent, they are the child.

About the Authors

Michael Lindsey, M.A. (Antioch University) has fifteen years' experience treating batterers. As co-founder of AMEND, he developed its clinical and administrative model. He is an expert witness in both civil and criminal domestic violence and stalking cases, trains criminal justice personnel and therapists working with perpetrators and victims of domestic violence, and is a community activist. He is currently director of The Third Path, a perpetrator treatment agency.

Robert W. McBride, M.B.A. (California State University at Fullerton) is a Certified Domestic Violence Councilor, has been involved in the domestic violence community ten years, and is currently working on an M.S.W. degree. He treated court-ordered addicted and violent men at Aurora Center for Treatment and is now with The Third Path. He teaches a course on domestic violence perpetrators at Metropolitan State College at Denver.

Constance M. Platt, Ph.D. (University of Denver) is information/public education coordinator for the Colorado Domestic Violence Coalition.

Index